T0194698

ALTERED

Discovering Unforeseen Joy through the Suffering That Has Drastically Altered Your Life

Eric Austin

WESTBOW
PRESS®
A DIVISION OF THOMAS NELSON
& ZONDERVAN

WestBow Press books may be ordered through booksellers or by contacting:

WestBow Press
A Division of Thomas Nelson & Zondervan
1663 Liberty Drive
Bloomington, IN 47403
www.westbowpress.com
844-714-3454

Because of the dynamic nature of the Internet, any web addresses or links contained in this book may have changed since publication and may no longer be valid. The views expressed in this work are solely those of the author and do not necessarily reflect the views of the publisher, and the publisher hereby disclaims any responsibility for them.

Any people depicted in stock imagery provided by Getty Images are models, and such images are being used for illustrative purposes only. Certain stock imagery © Getty Images.

A Grief Observed by CS Lewis © copyright CS Lewis Pte Ltd 1961.
The Problem of Pain by CS Lewis © copyright CS Lewis Pte Ltd 1940.
Used with permission.

Scripture quotations taken from the New American Standard Bible® (NASB), Copyright © 1960, 1962, 1963, 1968, 1971, 1972, 1973, 1975, 1977, 1995 by The Lockman Foundation Used by permission. www.Lockman.org

Scripture quotations marked (NIV) are taken from the Holy Bible, New International Version®, NIV®. Copyright © 1973, 1978, 1984, 2011 by Biblica, Inc.™ Used by permission of Zondervan. All rights reserved worldwide. www.zondervan.com The "NIV" and "New International Version" are trademarks registered in the United States Patent and Trademark Office by Biblica, Inc.™

THE NET BIBLE®, NEW ENGLISH TRANSLATION COPYRIGHT (c) 1996 BY BIBLICAL STUDIES PRESS, L.L.C. NET Bible® IS A REGISTERED TRADEMARK THE NET BIBLE® LOGO, SERVICE MARK COPYRIGHT (c) 1997 BY BIBLICAL STUDIES PRESS, L.L.C. ALL RIGHTS RESERVED

Scripture quotations are from the ESV® Bible (The Holy Bible, English Standard Version®), copyright © 2001 by Crossway, a publishing ministry of Good News Publishers. Used by permission. All rights reserved.

ISBN: 978-1-6642-2077-5 (sc)
ISBN: 978-1-6642-2078-2 (hc)
ISBN: 978-1-6642-2076-8 (e)

Library of Congress Control Number: 2021901196

Print information available on the last page.

WestBow Press rev. date: 3/22/2021

It is doubtful whether God can bless a man greatly until He has hurt him deeply.

—A. W. Tozer

CONTENTS

ACKNOWLEDGMENTS

First, before I could ever acknowledge all those I have leaned on for support, feedback, and encouragement to make this book come about, I have to thank my wife, Heidi. If not for her courage this book would never have been written. Although this is our story, she bears the burden of vulnerability in sharing it with the world. She takes such a great risk to herself in hopes that you, the reader, may find hope when all hope has failed and forever be radically altered by the grace of God. Heidi, thank you for your courage and your outrageous generosity in sharing how God has used some of your darkest moments.

Second, I am extremely grateful to Mindy Waltham, Lucas Grounds, and Josh Catania for their tremendous feedback on my manuscript. Also, thank you to those who read excerpts of the manuscript. Thank you to my good friend Stephen Scott and cousin Stephanie Longworth for their help in brainstorming cover design ideas. Thank you uncle Steve for suggesting the idea of writing a book over a round of golf. I still feel, as I did sitting in that golf cart, that very few will read it, but if one person would read it and be changed by our story then it will all be worth it. We would like to thank our counselor, Darcy McConnell, for her insight and direction throughout the years. Thank you for seeing beyond the crazy behavior to help us identify the unseen hurt driving it all.

Thanks to my mom and dad who, from as early as I can remember, built into me an overwhelming amount of self-confidence. You made me believe there was nothing I could not conquer though you knew there would be many obstacles and uncertainties waiting ahead of me. Thank you for also teaching me that giving up is never an option. Thank you to family and friends who got excited when I told them I was thinking of writing a book. I could have easily thrown in the towel on such an outrageous thought without everyone's belief in me and that the book would be a potential light to those suffering. Of course, thank you to our family for their continual support of us.

Finally, Heidi and I would like to apologize to anyone who may have been hurt by us over the years. Suffering is always messy and sadly our suffering has caused harm to some of you who were close. We are truly sorry and tell the truth that it has never been our intent to harm anyone. Things just spun out. If there is room at all to reconcile we are open to any and all.

BEFORE YOU READ

Before you read this book I have to say it may not be for you, at least it may not be right now. Your hurt might still be too fresh or your wound still gaping, if so do not read. Grieve. Punch a pillow. Scream. Breathe. Go through all five stages of grief two hundred times if you must. Find a friend who will sit with you and cry with you; find that person who will just be quiet, and listen to you. If you don't have that person then I pray God will send him or her along to you quickly.

C.S. Lewis wrote after the death of his wife, "Talk to me about the truth of religion and I'll listen gladly. Talk to me about the duty of religion and I'll listen submissively. But don't come talking to me about the consolations of religion or I shall suspect that you don't understand."[1] So, not to sound insincere, I want you to know along my own journey, I was told many consolations but I wasn't always ready to hear them. I was told many truths but I did not care to hear them. I just wanted the hurting to stop. That might be where you are right now. Many of those truths and comforts I was not ready to hear follow in this book. I understand, having gone through much myself, to have someone talk to you about how to handle your own suffering can come across insulting and calloused. So, before you read, know this book might not be for you right this moment. It is for those whom some of the chaos has calmed just enough hear and for those whom the tears have subsided just enough to see.

Only now, after almost a decade of suffering alongside my wife, stumbling our way through the perplexing and upside down world of mental illness, am I able to relay the truths and comforts that have sustained me when I felt I could no longer endure. Read when you are ready.

INTRODUCTION

Upstairs in the dark, a nine-year-old boy lay tucked in his red race car waterbed. On the school playground that day, the finger-pointing and the laughing were just too difficult to endure. Some days he was strong. Some days he wasn't. On his right side, he lay there crying softly, holding a small, brown, plastic, framed picture of a dirty-blonde hair Jesus with a manicured beard. You know the one where Jesus is quartered to the right and staring into the distance like a high school senior composite picture.

I lay there, holding it tightly, crying quietly so not to be heard. I prayed. I begged. I pleaded with God to cure me. To heal me. I told Him over and over that I knew He could fix me. I knew He was powerful enough to make my leg bend. I knew He could erase the physical scars of past surgeries. I knew He could make me walk and not grow weary and run and not feel faint. Oh man, I wanted to run on that playground and show those kids what was up. I knew He could make it all happen. I knew He could make me new. I knew He could quiet my haters. I quietly whispered these words between sobs until I fell asleep that night. I awakened the next morning to find the scars still there, my leg still fused straight, and my faith filled prayers unanswered.

What happens when God doesn't fix it? What happens when your life is turned upside down and inside out and God isn't answering the despairing midnight prayer? Twenty-five years since that nine-year-old boy's desperate plea for a miracle, the miracle still hasn't happened. This, however, does not mean God hasn't been working all this time toward a different outcome, a better outcome.

Now, for almost the last decade, my wife and I have endured a different kind of suffering: mental illness and the ensuing co-occurring alcohol abuse. Mental illness, along with its many co-occurring disorders, does not just alter a person; they alter marriages, friendships, careers, and lives. Suffering is an uninvited evil whose power drastically alters the lives of those within its crosshairs. It robs us of our sense of peace and often leaves our dreams for our own life decimated. I have no idea why God allows the suffering He does and so I definitely don't have the answer. I do, however, give you through the lens of our own suffering *an* answer to the very real hurt and confusion you feel as a believer in Jesus. I want to pass on what has been given to me when it seems God is more interested in being anywhere else other than listening your nighttime pleas. Through our story of suffering at the hands of borderline personality disorder and the alcohol abuse used to escape it, I hope to show you that although suffering drastically alters our lives, through it God, in His grace, stands ready to radically alter us. The outcome may not be what we ask, or even beg for, but in the end it is what we really want if we want to be like Jesus.

CHAPTER 1

The Dream Is Over

M Y FINGERS WRAPPED NERVOUSLY AROUND THE STEERING wheel, slightly tightening my already anxious grip. I couldn't tell you which was wrung tighter, the wheel or my stomach. The glaring pit sunk deeper. The enormous knot tighter. The lump in my throat grew wider as each anxious minute seemed to tick by shorter. *What was going to happen? What would I say?* I'm not really sure why I am making the drive to meet this girl. *How awkward will this be? What are we going to talk about? I mean she is pretty, but this makes the quasi-blind date all the more awkward.* Such were my skittish thoughts as the late January sun slowly slid lower to the west. As the horizon pulled down the fading sun, its rays pushed long shadows from leafless trees lining the rural highway. While I drove between the hypnotic back-and-forth flicker of light and shadow that had been thrust upon the road before me, the pit in my stomach grew; a pit that would eventually alter into something all too menacing and familiar in the years soon to come.

A mutual friend had set us up. He told me that she was

exactly like me and that we were perfect for each other. Well, she was actually the opposite of me in almost every way. She is an extrovert. I am an introvert. She loved to run. I couldn't run. She was the oldest of her siblings, and I was the youngest. She never stopped talking, and I preferred to quietly reflect. She is a tie-dyed-T-shirt-wearing, sunshine-is-always-shining type of girl who believes the glass is always half full, even when it's almost gone kind of girl. I'm a fly-under-the-radar type of guy.

I met Heidi during my undergrad years when Facebook had just rolled out and was only offered to a few universities. Adults were not able to create Facebook profiles until later. Facebook wasn't about community or connection back then as much as it was about stalking and creeping on people you knew. "Status" was a big deal. Whether you were in a relationship or not was a big deal. Posting how you felt or a picture of what you would eat definitely would have automatically led to ridicule back then. The best part of Facebook was "poking" people. No one really knew what it meant, though it acted as some weird virtual game of tag. So when my friend pulled Heidi up on Facebook and I saw her face, I thought, *Yeah, I could meet this girl.*

She went to school an hour from me, so I made the drive down the rural Oklahoma highway to take her out to dinner. She was more stunning in real life than she was on Facebook. (This was also a time when people didn't take a nauseating amount of pictures before posting the perfect one on social media.) That first date, I could not stop thinking of how beautiful she was. Her face was dressed with a warm smile that was disarming. Her skin glowed and she looked at me with the most optimistic brown eyes. She had a slight dimple, almost invisible, on the tip of her nose. The waves of her blonde hair fell past the front of her shoulders, framing perfectly her high cheeks and thin chin. I didn't like long hair, but I liked hers. At dinner she ordered a sweet potato as a side, which I thought was incredibly weird but also incredibly cute. Sweet potatoes are for Thanksgiving. It didn't matter, she was out of my league.

After dinner, I took her back to her apartment where I would drop her off. She asked me in after some of that awkwardness I had dreaded. We spent the rest of the evening watching *Iron Chef* and playing Mad Gab before I made the drive home. We actually had a lot of fun, but when asked the next day by my mom if there would be a second date, I remember my response was something like, "I'll probably never see her again." And that's exactly what happened for the next six months.

During that span of six months, another girl I had only met once at Whataburger in Florida started posting on my Facebook wall. After a while of this girl still not picking up on my disinterest, she posted on my wall, "I've decided that I just might be 'that' girl," which was odd because I didn't even know this girl. Before I could figure out a response, out of six months of silence, Heidi posted a reply. "How can she be 'that' girl when I am the girl?" A warm feeling swept over me, like the first catch of a cheesy childish crush. With it, I saw an opportunity. I cleverly suggested Heidi became my online girlfriend to fend off my clingy Facebook suitress. To my surprise, she agreed with little persuading and our status changed to "In a relationship." Come to find out, Heidi had an ex who thought he was still in the game which may be why she so easily agreed to our faux Facebook relationship. After a while, it came time for phase two of my clever plan, I would attempt to subtly move this Facebook relationship into a real relationship. That September I invited her on a second first date to a football game and for sushi. It only took two first dates, but we've never stopped dating.

She began making trips to visit me on the weekends. We would hang out with my friends. I quickly learned early on to never touch her face. I do not know when or how this fact came about, but it was made very clear to never touch her face. I agreed because her face was really pretty.

I remember the first time we held hands. We were walking through a friend's yard to the car when she stepped in a hole. I instinctively reached out to keep her from falling and our hands locked. Immediately there was this sort of surge that shot through me. A moment of anxiousness quickly washed away by excitement. We held hands the rest of the walk to the car. When she wasn't visiting on the weekends, she was mailing me letters enclosed in tie-dyed envelopes. I think she spent more time coloring the envelope with every color she had than she spent on the actual letter.

We dated a little over a year before getting engaged. My dad and I were driving down the road one day (to where I don't remember) when he asked me what it was I was waiting for. He made it clear I had done better than most thought I would with Heidi and should ask her to marry me before someone better came along for her. At least that's how I remember it. I thought he was right. I'd better seal the deal. I soon bought a ring.

Other than Heidi being beautiful, she had a beautiful side to her that I still, after ten years of marriage, cannot fully explain. During our engagement and early years of marriage, she would ask me, "What do you love most about me?" I never could give her a good answer; I could never explain fully what I loved most about her. I actually began to hate the question because I felt so bad I didn't have a definitive *"This* is why I love you ..." I always felt like I hurt her feelings, but I couldn't narrow my love down to, "Oh, I love you because you are so smart." or "... because you are so beautiful." Those reasons didn't fully capture why. So I'd always just sit there with a dumb look on my face and shrug my shoulders. Eventually, she stopped asking why I loved her and just took my word for it.

We married in July 2008 and moved to Dallas right before New Year's Day 2009. We didn't watch the ball drop that year. Instead, we sat on the floor of our new apartment binge-watching DVDs of *King of Queens* because we had no cable. I started seminary a few weeks later. In the meantime, Heidi was on the hunt for a job to pay the bills. The Great Recession had hit just a few months prior and jobs were not the easiest to come by those days. Heidi landed a temp job as an administrative assistant to the president of a fire protection company about seven minutes from our apartment. That doesn't happen in Dallas. A seven-minute commute—that's a miracle. Life was falling into place. God's face seemed to be smiling upon us; after all, I was going to seminary. God had to be good to us, right? Do good for God and God will do good for you?

Seminary began and I was convinced that I would change the world soon after. Four more years of education right after finishing four years of undergraduate work was a bit defeating, but the idea of changing the world motivated me. However, soon I realized just about everyone else in seminary thought they were going to be the one to change the world. It seemed everyone shared the same motivation as me, but everyone was smarter. They were better preachers than me. They were faster readers than me. They had better personalities than me. I was obscured in the one place I thought I would stand out.

It was after my first sermon assignment that Heidi and I watched the video of my preaching. It was so painful to watch and hear. Oh, my eyes and my ears. I still cringe, even now, when I think back to the haunting homiletics displayed in that video. I was extremely discouraged. As we discussed the sermon and how discouraged I was in general with seminary, Heidi flat out said, "You're not smart. You just try really hard." A hush fell across our small living room. A silence you might expect before a storm or a great battle. It didn't come across the way she intended, but it wasn't worth trying to walk back at this point. She sat there looking at me, wondering if I was going to explode.

I was ready to snap at her, to shield my severe insecurity, when it dawned on me that she was right. Nothing had ever come easily in my life. I have always had to give extra effort. I was told I would never walk. I had to figure that out. If I wanted to keep up with the neighborhood kids, I needed to figure out how to ride a bike with a leg that couldn't bend. If I wanted to go to college one day and not have my mom move in with me, I had to figure out how to put a sock on my foot. (Putting a sock on is tough when you can't touch your toes.)

Heidi was right. It hurt when she said it, but she was right and my optimism had been restored. I was going to be the scrappy seminarian. Heidi always tells me what I need to hear, not what I want to hear. There is nothing more valuable as a leader, husband, dad, or mom than to have the truth told to you, no matter how badly it may hurt. The only thing more valuable, I guess, would be to have the humility to hear it. Thankfully that day I had it. It's not always a guarantee. Thankfully, this also would not be the last time Heidi would help me with my sermons.

WHEN MAYHEM STRIKES

The following semester, Heidi came to class to be interviewed by me to close a sermon. The short sermon began with a YouTube video of an Allstate Insurance "Mayhem" commercial to illustrate how life can blindside us at any moment. The commercial raised the question. "What will you do when Mayhem strikes?" I used that one commercial where Mayhem is in the woman's blind spot as she drives down the highway. She turns her head to check her driver's side mirror. Mayhem looks back at the woman in her mirror. With a warm, but mischievous smile and a thumbs up, he tells her, "You're good." She changes lanes. *Bam!* A big truck with a large grille guard smashes her blindside, sending her car into a slow-motion spin with her screaming while Mayhem laughs on deep and sinisterly. I saw it one night and couldn't stop laughing.

So I opened with Mayhem. The stagnate classroom was mostly empty except for the four other students, primed and ready to critique. The room remained quiet with only the sound of softly rustling papers. My turn came. I preached hesitantly, faking it while hoping I would make it good enough for a B. I'd take a C. I was disheveled in my appearance. My hair looked like I combed it the night before, cowlick in back raging full force. I wore a five o'clock shadow at 9:00 a.m., dress jeans, and an untucked white button-up draping out from underneath my black, velvet dress coat. My preaching was not dressed much better. After ten minutes of the painful exposition, I brought Heidi on stage for her to share her story. She takes us back a few months to the beginning of the semester when mayhem had blindsided her. And me.

Months earlier I had taken Heidi to the doctor because of intense abdominal pain. They discovered two cysts on her ovaries, one the size of a golf ball and the other a baseball. Heidi soon after had surgery and a biopsy performed. She went in for her follow-up appointment where she found out she had polycystic ovarian syndrome (PCOS). Heidi was blindsided by the news that her hopes of a baby and family one day had been reduced to 1 percent. If she wanted to get pregnant, it would be a long road not without the help of modern medicine. Even then, after the long road, there was no guarantee of a child.

Heidi was strong as she navigated her way home through the congested traffic of Dallas/Fort Worth. Once home, I hear the door slowly close followed by the heavy sad thud of her steps as she comes up the stairs. Once to the top of the stairs she walks into our now not so new apartment. I see her face as she looks up at me. I don't know this face. On it she wore a dejected sadness I had not seen before. Without command, her purse slides off her shoulder and down her arm crashing to the floor. As our eyes meet she begins to cry.

The morning of my sermon, Heidi quietly ascends the one or two steps up to the mini stage in my classroom. I pulled up two classroom chairs with desktops connected. I'm almost certain these chairs had been around since the 1960s. The interview begins. I'm trying to use my body language to show I'm engaged, but I look like a hunchback leaned forward, arms extended straight out and draped over the desk as if to keep me from further falling over. Much of the time I'm looking down as if to suggest I'm deep in thought, but really, without meaning to, I gesticulate boredom. It was bad. But Heidi did great. She was a natural. My professor had plenty of tips for me, but his only comment for Heidi was that she was a natural. And she really was. She saved the sermon. She brought it home for me. She ended her story by answering my last question. "How do you keep on trusting God in the midst of Mayhem?" Seven years later, as the mayhem of Heidi's self-destructive behavior is about to kill me, literally feeling like I can go on no longer, I hear the lyrics of Elevation Worship's song "Do It Again," which echoed the same sentiments of Heidi's answer seven years earlier to close out my sermon. "I keep on trusting because He's never failed me yet."

Although we had been blindsided by Heidi's polycystic ovarian syndrome, we were still living the dream. We were three years into marriage. Most tell us their first years of marriage were the hardest, but they were the best for us. We were living in the Dallas/Fort Worth area where there are countless fun things to do, see, and eat. We had become incredible foodies. There is so much good food in Dallas it is unbelievable. The problem was the food was expensive and we were on a tight budget. No worries. We found a loophole. Virtually everywhere in Dallas has a happy hour. If you sit in the bar or on the patio, appetizers are half price before 6:30 p.m., some places 7:00. The next problem was that the drinks were also inexpensive. Everything was fine, though. I was focused on why we were in Dallas. I was still taking a crazy amount of credit hours and spending hours in the library, so happy hour was just that, a happy time that both Heidi and I could be together for the first time all day. We talked about everything while playing Scrabble, passing the phone back and forth across the table. Everything was fine.

So I thought.

During these years in Dallas, Heidi was not fine. In December

2008, Heidi had graduated with her master's degree in Nutritional Sciences right before moving to Dallas. However, due to the economic climate around the country, corporate wellness type jobs were first to be cut. Heidi settled for all she could get, a temp job at a fire protection company to be the breadwinner. She worked nine to five for us while I took on seminary full time.

This day-in and day-out routine of nine to five left Heidi with an existential boredom that created a deep angst within, leaving her feeling overcome with a sad sense of no real purpose beyond making us money. Working as a temp for a fire protection company after working so hard to earn her master's degree felt like a major setback in those early days. Although she loves her job and finds a great deal of satisfaction in her work now, those early days were hard on her.

Martin Seligman, known by many as the father of positive psychology, proposed that a person's ability to deal with setbacks in life is largely determined by his of her explanatory style. He writes,

> Your habitual way of explaining bad events, your explanatory style, is more than just the words you mouth when you fail. It is a habit of thought, learned in childhood and adolescence. Your explanatory style stems directly from your view of your place in the world—whether you think you are valuable and deserving, or worthless and hopeless.[2]

There are three dimensions to everyone's explanatory style: permanence, pervasiveness, and personalization.

Permanence has to do with time. A person will bounce back from a bad event more quickly if he or she doesn't view their setback as lasting permanently. The one who gives up easily is one who thinks of time in absolutes using words like *always*. They say things, such as "This *always* happens to me" or "I *never* catch a break" or "My team *never* wins." As a result of this habit of thought, the setback feels like it is permanent and their present is as good as it will ever get. They feel stuck or trapped, not because of their setback but because of their habit of thought. When a person is unable to see anything else for their future, they may have fallen victim to permanence. They honestly feel like the setback will always be. If you are a victim of permanence, then you know the helplessness and hopelessness that can easily engulf you.

Whereas permanence has to do with time, pervasiveness has to do with space. This person who does not bounce back from a setback quickly views the cause for their setback as universal. As a result, the person feels helpless in all areas of life. However, a person who views the explanation to their setback as specific to their particular setback will rebound more quickly, feeling less helpless. This person will continue to excel in other areas of their life, understanding their failure as limited or specific to the one event. When something goes wrong a person will either view the setback as permeating into other aspects of life or contained to the event itself. A mom who may have a negative pervasive explanatory style might think, *I'm a terrible mom*, when all she did was forget the diaper bag at home.

The final dimension is personalization. Personalization is different from permanence and pervasiveness in that personalization results in how you feel because of your setback, whereas the previous two control how you will respond to your setback. Personalization has to do with internalizing or externalizing the cause for a setback. People who tend to view themselves as unlovable or worthless will internalize. The one who internalizes will blame their setback on themselves. When a failure occurs, these individuals will say things such as "I'm not smart enough" or "I'm not good enough." In other words, the person shames himself or herself. A person, however, who externalizes, places the blame on others to redirect attention away from themselves because, in my opinion, they fear being seen as unlovable or worthless. "You're stupid" or "This is all your fault" are the types of comments and thoughts of those who externalize.

It is all too easy to blame yourself or others for life's setbacks. It is easy to let your thoughts develop into a thought life where failures feel permanent and pervasive. Some of you may feel empty even now. Your work lacks a bigger mission; you just push paper and crunch numbers for a boss, not for a bigger cause. Life without a higher calling is dangerous. Our thought life—how we respond in our thinking to our setbacks in life—is crucial.

Perhaps you once believed your life would be more impacting than it appears. You thought you were going to make a big splash but most days you feel invisible, even useless. You beat yourself up over past decisions. Perhaps the setback that has blindsided you has you responding in ways you never dreamed you would behave. It feels like year after year nothing changes.

Year after year, nothing changed for Heidi. These feelings led to a deeper angst and heightened anticipation to find her escape in the murky waters of happy hour. Happy hour for Heidi had not just become an escape from the humdrum mundane routine of purposelessness, but it was her false sense of connection and escape from the unsettling feeling that she was amounting to nothing significant. It was a way to redirect externally from the internal agony and self-harassment resulting from her own perceived personal failings.

Heidi would later tell me that happy hour had also become the great equalizer. It didn't matter if you were the CEO of a major company or an administrative assistant; everyone at happy hour was equal as far as appearances went. In her mind, she could pretend to be like everyone else. Everyone there is important, relaxing from an intense day at the office. Mix in the chemical effects of alcohol to the brain chemistry and memory connections being associated during these happy times at these happy hours, and we've got a real problem being masked.

I had no idea, but increasingly over the years while in Dallas, there were warning signs that a big problem was looming over us, becoming more visible and sinister each year. However, when I would take notice I cunningly convinced myself that no danger threatened. It was as if I were looking into my own driver's side mirror with Mayhem smiling right back at me giving me the thumbs up, comforting me with the words, "You're good!"

During these years in Dallas as Heidi's drinking began to rev up, unknown to us in the shadowy recesses of her personality, a disorder was revving up as well. It was emerging in her and we hadn't the slightest clue. This personality disorder would intensify and worsen over the next nine years before being diagnosed. In the meantime, all I, or anyone else, could see was the alcohol abuse that manifested on the outside to cope. Heidi was sinking into the upside down world of borderline personality disorder.

Borderline personality disorder or BPD is referred to by many as an "emotion dysregulation." BPD centers on one's inability to manage emotions and impulsivity. Like many who suffer from BPD, Heidi's inability to manage volatile emotions, such as shame and anger, can result in co-occurring disorders like substance abuse, eating disorders, and major depressive disorder. As Heidi's BPD went untreated for years her self-destructive tendencies worsened. Also, the impulsivity that is so characteristic of borderline, became near impossible for her to control when she became dysregulated.

It would be years before we even hear the words "borderline personality disorder." For now, it is May. I'm finally to the day I thought would never come. I'm graduating. The day, however, was bittersweet. Just a week earlier, mayhem blindsided us again, but worse. Heidi had her first miscarriage. As blindsiding as the news of PCOS was, the miscarriage was much more. Neither of us really processed the loss of our baby. I was graduating and Heidi repressed the unmanageable hurt by coordinating with family coming to town for commencement chapel then the commencement ceremony the following day. The week was honestly a blur leading up to commencement. Then the week after graduating, Heidi's family took us to Belize for a family vacation. We got back home late Wednesday night, and Thursday afternoon I am going in for an emergency appendectomy. Looking back, we did not process the loss well or even at all.

Like most people, we never even considered the chance of a miscarriage. We didn't know one in four women is at risk. We had thought the struggle would be conceiving a baby, not carrying a baby. That day began like any other day. We woke up. She saw a little spotting but didn't think anything of it. I went down the street to get a haircut. She had called her doctor just to let them know. They told her to come in to check things out. So she made the fifteen-minute drive over to Grapevine to get checked out. Meanwhile, I'm back in Irving leaving after finishing my haircut. I get to my car to see a text message, "Come to the doctor's office now."

The drive down the highway that morning was calm. No radio. No traffic. I thought something bad had happened but didn't really let my thoughts run wild. I arrive and walk straight toward the check-in counter.

"I'm with Heidi Austin." As soon as I say the words, without hesitation, a door opens. *Never a good sign,* I remember thinking. On the other side of the door waiting for me was a serious woman, fitted in scrubs.

"Right this way," she said softly.

I follow the woman quietly to a door at the end of a long, sterile, florescent white hallway. As we make the lonely walk the tension in me grew heavier as the door drew nearer. She opens the door to a softly lit room where Heidi looks up at me with her heavy brown eyes. Her face is dressed in that dejected sadness I had not come accustom to yet. The tears coursed over and down her cheeks to her chin where the back of her hand quietly erased them before they fell. The look on her sullen face, I swear, sucked all the air out of the room. She didn't need to say it. She didn't need to say anything. I knew right then we had lost the baby.

Everyone tells you how to be a good husband, but no one prepares you to be a good husband in crisis. After what seemed like an enormous pause, I finally inhaled; and not knowing what to say I went straight to her. I didn't speak, I just listened, as she told me everything that happened between the sobs, moment by moment, from when she sat down, to the look on the technician's face, to the comforting words the technician gave her after the tragic news. I told her I would never miss another sonogram again. And I didn't. Mayhem had struck, and this time it left death.

~~TEN-YEAR PLAN~~

Three years after graduating seminary, I sat in a booth for breakfast across from an elder at the church where I had been on staff in Oklahoma. The restaurant was polluted by the warm smell of greasy bacon and half cooked hash browns. At this particular breakfast, he asked me if I had given any thought to my ten-year plan. Between my bites of over-easy eggs and sips of coffee, I explained that in ten years I would like to be a lead pastor of a church. Before then, perhaps in two to three years, I wished to transition out of student ministry into teaching adults. I knew I also needed to grow more in church administration and leadership during this time. As any young and wide-eyed twenty-something feels as they embark upon their career, I felt a lot of hope and excitement for my future.

Two years after that breakfast, I sat in a booth across from the same man for breakfast in the same bacon sullied restaurant. The same marked air of greasy bacon and half cooked hash browns lingered as it did years before, but everything else had changed. I had just arrived back in town after having left Heidi in rehab. Having to know I was discouraged, he invited me to breakfast. Two years earlier at our breakfast, we had talked about my ten-year plan. This breakfast, we talked about grief. And, what I didn't know at the time, was also the looming and quickly coming loss of my own dream.

I understand grief to be the suffering of some sort of loss. In my case, the loss of how I thought my life was going to go. My marriage. My ministry. My mission. My ten-year plan. I naïvely thought I was going to change the world after seminary, remember? This man was a recently retired professor in the Department of Communication Sciences and Disorders at the university in town. He told me how he used to teach a section to his students over grief. In our conversation, he shared how he taught students that everyone has "dreams" about how their life is supposed to turn out, but when a mom finds out her dream baby is deaf, sometimes the grief is too much to bear.

He told a story of a mother who had been all over to see countless doctors, desperately chasing a second, a third, and a fourth opinion for her child. Every time the news was the same. "Ma'am, your child is deaf." She wouldn't have it. She couldn't accept it. She was unwilling to let go of her dream. She was unwilling to let go of the way she had always pictured her children and her family. She never pictured a deaf child. Her life had been drastically altered, and she was unwilling to accept it. This mom needed to wake up to the fact that her dream was over. Life had handed her something entirely different than she had planned. She was blindsided for sure, but she needed to wake up to the reality that her child was indeed deaf.

Like this devastated mother, you may need to wake up as well and accept that the dream is over. Life as you had pictured it will not happen entirely or perhaps at all now. If you are reading this, there is a good chance you are suffering or a loved one is suffering in some way. You may have lost your job. You may have lost your marriage. Perhaps you yourself are struggling with the existential boredom Heidi felt in Dallas and coping with it in all the wrong ways. Perhaps those close to you keep telling you you're not yourself lately and you need to talk with a counselor. A loved one of yours may be abusing pills. Maybe you are finding yourself abusing alcohol. That beer after work has turned into ultimatums from your spouse or probation from your boss. Life is altering into something you never dreamed of for yourself. The first thing you need to do is wake up. Whatever has hit you to drastically alter your life I'm sure did not fit into your ten-year plan, but the longer you hold on to *your* dream, the longer you will miss out on God's dream. It is time to surrender *your* dream life for *His* dream for your life.

You and I never would have chosen this calling, but this is our calling. The God of the universe is calling us into a messy, wild adventure of suffering and grace; rejection and redemption. I know you may not like the sound of being called to suffer. Yet sin has fouled up everything. Sin has fouled up your loved one's mind, your dream, your finances, or perhaps your friendships. Since it has fouled up everything, suffering is now inescapable. The suffering that is inescapable is wreaking havoc in your life, and worst of all, you know it has forever altered your life in some way. I get it. Believe me, I do. You are angry that God is not delivering on the dream life you trusted Him for. Now is the time to begin accepting that the dream is over. Your life has been drastically altered, and God has a different outcome for your life than you originally conjured. The outcome may be different than you originally dreamed, but still an outcome amazing and beyond what you could have ever dreamed for yourself. He wants to leverage the suffering that has drastically altered your life to radically alter you.

At that time, when we sat for breakfast and discussed grief, two years earlier I had hoped to be transitioning in my career as a pastor, but in just three months I would no longer even be a pastor. My ten-year plan was gone. God had crossed it out. He put a big fat line right through it. Accepting the loss of a dream, however, has been beyond the best thing we could have dreamed to happen for ourselves. And it will be the same for you too.

Maybe you need to cross out your ten-year plan as well. Maybe you need to put a big fat line through it and accept a different plan, God's plan for you. God sent His one and only Son to die and live again so your dream life could die and you truly live for Him. Hopefully, by reading our wild story, you'll find that God desires to use your suffering to radically alter your life into something you never dreamed it could be. One day, God willing, you will find yourself thanking God for your suffering because it has made you more like Jesus and there is no greater unforeseen joy you can experience than that. You will sound like the psalmist who wrote, "It is good for me that I was afflicted, that I may learn Your statutes" (Psalm 119:71 NASB).

CHAPTER 2

You Promised You Were Done

D ENIAL IS A WEIRD THING. IT REMINDS ME A LOT OF MY TWIN girls when we play hide-and-seek. When we play, both girls will cover their eyes with their hands so they can't see me. They think that if they can't see me, then I must not be able to see them. Covering their eyes, in their minds, acts like some invisibility cloak that protects them from my tickles. But it doesn't! Covering your eyes to the full reality of suffering does not hide you from it either. Denial does not shelter you nor protect you from the scary reality of suffering's life-altering implications. It only creates more hurt, more of the very hurt you are desperately trying to avoid. Denial might feel safe in our minds; it may seem to wrap warmly around us, comforting us and soothing us, but it does not.

As I neared the end of seminary, I had myself completely convinced once I got a job and we moved, Heidi would snap out of her increasingly erratic behavior. A new environment and culture would bring a new lifestyle. Ultimately, however, I couldn't reconcile the fun, outgoing, glass-half-full, tie-dyed-T-shirt-wearing girl I knew, with the behavior I was seeing. That girl was disappearing, and I could not stop it. It was like trying to hold onto water.

We had not been in Oklahoma very long before I realized the new environment was not helping Heidi. It became all too clear it was actually making things worse. We didn't know it then but environment can be a major trigger for BPD. So much of how we feel comes from our environment. The people, places, smells, sounds, and the memories associated with these environments all bring about certain emotions, good and bad, in us all; but at times these emotions might be too overwhelming for the borderline. We moved from a big city to a tiny town and into a tiny 805-square-foot, two-bed, one-bath apartment. They were the same apartments we lived in the first six months we were married before moving to Dallas. The small town youth pastor wife role Heidi stepped into created an unbearable amount of anxiety. The only way she knew how to escape the inescapable emotions that overwhelmed her was what she had learned in Dallas—drink.

I didn't know what she was drinking though. Her drinking was secretive, perhaps she felt being a pastor's wife and drinking was taboo. While Heidi slept off the mystery drinks, I began a bad habit of my own—hunting. I became obsessed with needing to know what and how she was drinking behind my back. I knew whatever it was, by this point, it was in the apartment and I just had to find it.

One evening I put Heidi to bed and commenced my mystery drink hunt. With Heidi almost comatose in our bed under the full brightness of our fluorescent lights, I opened the bifold closet doors in our bedroom. You know the ones that fold open like an accordion to both the left and right. I swung the doors open with bravado. I had gotten good at finding her stashes by this point. She was running out of places in our 805 square feet.

I survey the mess of clothes that had been tried on and discarded to the floor days earlier. The clutter of clothes deemed unfitting and strung out was a graveyard of women's shoes buried beneath its surface. The closets in our apartment were tiny so I took the second bedroom closet for my clothes. So to be clear this was not my mess. I get down on all four. I dig in. I know something is in there. I'm learning her patterns. I know she can't outsmart me forever. Eventually, I'll root out every hiding place she can think of and this will all be over. I knew exactly what I was looking for. And I found it.

Tennis shoes, dress shoes, heels—there was a pair on that closet floor for every occasion. I slowly shuffled through them until I uncovered a water bottle with red wine in it. I found it. I took the bottle into the living room. I set it on the coffee table where she would see it once she walked out. I sat down on the edge of our couch and waited. And waited.

Finally, she awakened, lucid she came out of the bedroom.

"Look what I found," I tout proudly.

"What's that?" she asks, as she looks at the bottle with phony bewilderment.

"What do you think it is? It's your secret wine."

"That's not mine. I don't do that anymore. It must be from weeks ago."

She's dismissive in tone as she turns to walk away. My voice raises.

"Don't walk away from me! I know you're drinking."

Redirecting she asks, "Where did you even find that?"

I know better than to tell her. She may have another bottle neatly tucked away that I want her to lead me to.

"It doesn't matter where I found it. I found it, and you promised you were done!"

"I am done, Eric!"

"Why do you lie to me? You're still a little drunk right now!"

"Whatever," she mumbles as she turns back for bed.

Multiple times I found her shoe wine stashed in her closet, and multiple times before that she promised she was done. Finding the stashes after the fact wasn't solving anything. She clearly wasn't going to stop so I had to stop her before she could drink. My role in our marriage had become the *foiler*. I took the responsibility upon myself to foil any plan she had of drinking. This was not a healthy role, of course. At night I was so stressed about what was happening to Heidi or what was hidden in the apartment that I started clenching and grinding my teeth as I slept. After a while, I ground a canine tooth down. The dental hygienist even asked me about my stress level at one cleaning. Things were becoming more out of control. But I continued to shield myself with denial.

I take showers like the rest of decent nonstinky human beings. For most, showers are a relaxing ten minutes out of the day. No screaming children. No phone calls. No work. Forget all that. Showers had become extremely stressful for me. I dreaded them. My showers had turned into opportunities for Heidi. I showered as fast as I possibly could if I thought there was a new stash in the apartment. The fear of her getting into it and hurting herself was so much that I could hardly leave her side.

The only time in which I could find rest during this period of our marriage was when I was right next to her in a place I knew she could not fool me. This led us to isolate ourselves from family and friends. I had to always be by Heidi. I had to always have the ability to control the environment. I had to be the *foiler*.

In the meantime, I kept buying time; I kept deceiving myself, telling myself this problem had to be a fluke or a phase of immature drinking. Perhaps, it is all just a curious case of not careful consumption. I would find any reason to not fully believe what I already knew deep down. I would tell myself that her perspective on drinking is a product of how she was raised. Her mother taught her and her sisters how to shop and find good bargains. This bargain mentality has warped how she viewed alcohol. If she drinks it fast, she won't need to pay for another one.

Another justification I regularly deceived myself with was Heidi's education. Heidi had her bachelor's degree in Exercise Physiology and her master's degree in Nutritional Sciences. I told myself countless times she drinks fast so she doesn't have to consume more calories. She's just budgeting her caloric intake. This would pass. Eventually, she would see the negative consequences and realize this behavior isn't worth it. It isn't worth the fights, the hangovers, and the embarrassment. It isn't worth losing respect from friends and family. I was doubling down on my denial hoping it all would soon pass. The result, though, was sustaining and strengthening a cycle of betrayal and anxiety.

Deep down, however, I knew she had a very scary problem and I knew I sounded crazy most of the time with my justifications, but I couldn't stop. I couldn't face what I knew to be true. Like the devastated mother, I was chasing down second, third, and fourth opinions. I didn't want to believe she had an alcohol abuse problem because I knew it would change our lives forever. This type of problem doesn't fit in ministry. This type of problem doesn't fit our calling. This type of problem doesn't fit in our town. The reality that Heidi had an alcohol abuse problem hurt, and I didn't want to hurt. I wanted it all to go away. Denial kept me safe from the suffocating hurt that our life, as we knew it, was over.

So why did I continue to make excuses and rationalize signs of significant alcohol abuse? I mean shoe wine is not exactly a thing. They have appropriate places for wine like cellars, coolers, bottles, and racks, but not in water bottles buried under stinky shoes in tiny closets. I continued in my denial because I thought it gave me a sense of peace and would protect me from having to face the scary world of substance abuse and mental illness. I thought it would buy me time until she would come to her senses. Snap out of it. Or just get bored with it all. God was not supposed to allow this kind of thing to happen to us.

You might be thinking something similar. *God isn't supposed to allow this to happen.* Suffering, in general, betrays some sense of how we believe our world should work. Ultimately, the news of grief betrays a belief we hold how God Himself should work. Sometimes we don't know how to reconcile a good God with our messed up world not operating the way we believe it ought to, so denial acts as our protector. It protects us from hurt. It acts to protect our sense of peace. It even protects us from our God. It is scary to think the world isn't what we've grown up believing it is. It is scary to think God doesn't always work how we've grown up believing He should. It is scary to think that God's plan for us may actually include suffering.

Denial is our Tarshish, it is a safe place we run to so we don't have to face the scary, life-altering reality God is calling us to face. And that's what I did. I ran. That's what we all do. Perhaps you are desperately covering your eyes, hoping you will be draped with some invisibility cloak. You feel denying it somehow shelters you from the glaring pain you don't want to face. And, after waiting long enough, when you open your eyes it will all be gone. It will pass by. But it won't. You cannot deny reality forever and not get hurt.

DEFEATED HERO

When I was in high school, I loved music. I would play my guitar and drums in my room for hours. Music was definitely a way I coped with the teenage angst of the 1990s. I like bands of all stripes. As a child of the 1990s, I was naturally a fan of alternative/grunge rock. I rocked out with Kurt Cobain of Nirvana. Gavin Rossdale of Bush and I performed duets of "Glycerin" for the ladies. I loved nerd rock like Weezer and Ben Folds Five. Wilco and Death Cab for Cutie were top indie bands for me. In the early 2000s, I became a fan of Jimmy Eat World. I loved blaring "Sweetness" with the windows down in my white Ford Explorer as an insecure and overcompensating sixteen-year-old. Their album *Futures* was released later while I was in college. One song on that album I listened to a lot, in particular, was "Drugs or Me." Back then I never thought much about it other than it was really catchy.

Fast-forward a decade, I've just picked up lunch to take to the preschool to eat with my four-year-old son for Hero Day. As I'm driving, I plug my phone in to charge, and "Drugs or Me" comes through the car speakers. *Sweet. I haven't heard this song in years,* I thought. I start listening, and it's not long into the song when I lose it. I can't stop the tears. I'm enveloped, inescapably, and completely engulfed; I am drenched in an array of utter sadness. It now was a completely different song than ten years earlier. I feel as if Heidi were lost somehow or as if some stranger had taken her—no, taken over her. I was sad for Heidi. I was sad for me. I was sad for our son. I was sad for the Eric who listened to the song years earlier and had not a clue to the hurt barreling toward him.

I don't know, but I'm pretty sure the song is a conversation between an addict and a person who loves him or her deeply. Again, I don't know, but here are just a few lines from the song. It may sound familiar.

> If only you could see
> The stranger next to me
> You promise, you promise that you're done
> But I can't tell you from the drugs
>
> I wish that you could see
> This face in front of me
> You're sorry, you swear it, you're done
> But I can't tell you from the drugs

I sat in my car outside of my son's preschool on Hero Day, just staring out the window toward the playground strewed with tiny toys and play equipment, feeling so dejected. Feeling so defeated. The song somehow miraculously shed enough scales from my eyes to gain a clear glimpse into years of hurtful betrayal allowed by my denial. Years of hurt I've pretended weren't really happening. The words in the song felt as if they had been recklessly ripped right out of the pages of my own life. Just a day earlier, we stood in our kitchen and I didn't even recognize Heidi. I didn't recognize the face that was looking back at me. The stranger's eyes were dead and hung lazily as she tried to focus on me. It was more than I could bear. The anger. The fear. The sense that everything was out of control overtook me in the kitchen.

"You promised you were done!" I screamed.

She remains focused, squinting her heavy brown eyes at me as if I were an anchor to keep her from swaying too far to the left or right.

"How does this keep happening?" I yell.

I rail against her for the next thirty minutes straight. I rarely came up for breath. I finally stop because I about pass out from not breathing between my verbal blows. The more this happens, the more personal it feels. She knows how much this hurts me, but my happiness is not enough to deter her. Our happiness isn't enough to restrain her. After all this, she remains resolute in her commitment to refresh her borderline impulsive indulgences at my expense. With every act of deceit, the hurt of betrayal grows deeper; with every lie that comes out of her mouth, the resentment rises exponentially higher.

If substance abuse has altered your loved one in some way, you too have felt this intense betrayal. You too have had your share of outbursts. You too have looked into the deadness of your loved one's eyes, which were once filled with so much life and now filled with so much morose, and yelled, "You promised you were done!" The person who has used and stands in front of us is not our son. She's not our daughter. The person is not our husband or wife. It is some stranger next to us. After a while, they don't even need to be under the influence for us to not recognize them. It is utterly terrifying.

This terror isn't just reserved for those suffering from a loved one's substance abuse or addiction. It is the terror we all feel when suffering betrays our belief of how life is supposed to be. It is the terror we feel as we watch our child lying in a hospital bed weak as the cancer eats away. It is felt when we don't recognize our spouse who is declining rapidly from ALS. Or when a parent who suffers from Alzheimer's doesn't recognize us anymore. We become so scared we will do anything to get them back. We will pay whatever ransom necessary. That payment is usually made in our time, energy, and money. Like any loving mom, dad, wife, or friend, we will do anything to save our loved one.

The *real* betrayal, however, isn't when we are promised things like sobriety, loyalty, and fidelity and they don't turn out. The real betrayal isn't when the doctor has said a year earlier the cancer is gone, but your child lies weak in bed again from chemo. The real betrayal is that your child *is* lying in that bed in the first place. It's not supposed to be this way at all. The real betrayal *is* life not being what it was meant to be. What you dreamed it to be. What it is supposed to be. What you trusted God for it to be. We were not created to suffer, yet here we are. Deep down, whether you are a believer in Jesus or not, you know suffering is an injustice and we are meant for more. This is why we all so desperately want it to end.

I walked into the preschool with lunch that Hero Day a defeated hero. Heroes save people. I was more like a powerless poser who thought by making excuses I could save Heidi's reputation. I thought the excuses would buy her time until she snapped out of it. By doubling down on my denial, I wasn't saving Heidi as I thought. I wasn't her hero. My denial was hurting her. It was hurting me. It was hurting our son. I had to face the hurt that the world as I thought it should be—as I believed it was meant to be—had betrayed me. It can happen at any moment; the world, as we believe it is supposed to be, betrays us. Life, as we assume it ought to be is drastically altered forever. A shooter enters a school. You answer the ringing phone. A driver plows into a crowd. At that moment, your life is forever altered.

SHE'S BLACK AND MEDEVACS

We live in a small town with a big university. Every fall, usually in October, the university has its annual homecoming festivities and along with them a parade. The parade runs up Main Street and ends at the cross street, Hall of Fame. We sat down toward the end of the parade route in front of the Sonic Drive-In, about three hundred yards from where the parade finished at Hall of Fame. The parade had just ended when we heard sirens—a lot of sirens. It was only a matter of minutes before fire engines and ambulances were trying to maneuver through the post parade traffic in front of us. From where we were standing, we couldn't make out exactly what was going on down at the intersection of Main and Hall of Fame, but people walking from that direction said that a car hit some people. Every year as soon as the end of the parade passes by, people start crossing the street on foot. Cars pull out and drive at a snail's speed, so I assumed if a car hit someone, it barely clipped them and the injuries were minor.

I was in my third year as the student pastor at a church in

town. Some of our teens had been in the parade so I thought I'd better at least walk down and make sure none of our kids were hurt. As I get closer, I realize by the way people are hustling this isn't an accident with minor injuries. I walk up to the intersection and notice it is littered with debris, blankets, chairs, and bodies. A lot of bodies. Moments ago, off-duty nurses and doctors were paradegoers, but now—along with first responders—they had become mini makeshift trauma teams huddled over countless people.

Police tape draped from each corner of the intersection tied to the traffic light poles, creating a perimeter guarded by national guardsmen. These same guardsmen had just finished marching in the parade moments before a car came barreling into the crowd that lined the intersection. I walk up to one of the guardsmen to let him know I am a pastor and available if any family members needed someone to sit with or help find loved ones who may have been lost in the chaos. He tells me to stay put and he walks off as if to find someone.

As I wait, I look down and see ten feet from me a body covered by a tarp. The cool gentle autumn breeze gusts a bit, just enough to lift the edge of the tarp back for me to see a man's face. Then I look up and realize that they had now taped off a wider perimeter with me in it. As I wonder if I should step out of the taped-off area, I realize that the gentle autumn breeze that picked up just moments ago was actually the air beginning to stir as the medevacs started their descent. The trees lining the street tossed violently back and forth as two medevacs slowly landed. Responders swiftly moved the critical to the choppers. They lifted off and once cleared then two more medevacs circling would come down. These choppers had to be coming from all over the state. As I stood there, chaos unfolding all around me, I remember thinking, *This doesn't feel like my small town. It feels like a war zone.* It was like a bomb had been lit in the middle of a crowd, sending people every which direction, and we are all left frantically picking up the pieces.

I snapped out of my daze of disbelief at the unfolding scene around me to hear a responder say, "She's black and we've got more reds." I thought, *She's black? What in the world does that mean? Does that mean she's dead?* The national guardsman returns with a police officer. The officer tells me to go to the other side of the intersection where the families are being told to meet. I head toward the rendezvous point but quickly realize I can't get to the other side because the whole area has been taped off. I go back to the police officer to let her know I can't get to the other side of the intersection. She lifts the tape and begins leading me through the carnage from one corner of the intersection to its opposite.

I'm taking it all in as I walk by people who have just been plowed into by a car. As I walk through the bodies, mangled and left to writhe on the cool asphalt by the driver, I have to maneuver carefully around the debris and some slimy red gelatin on the pavement. It would be three years later after the emergency responders lift Heidi's body off our tile floor, that I would recognize the red gelatin as coagulation.

I kept moving through the intersection behind the officer and spotted another lumped blanket. As I walk by I see a woman's still and cooling hand just outside the edge of the blanket covering her. A hand that may once have spontaneously held another's for the first time. A hand that warmly held a child or grandchild tightly. A hand that now would never hold again. *Will I be the person to have to talk to her family members on the other side of this intersection?*

It just takes a moment and our world can be completely flipped upside down. Our lives can be drastically and forever altered like the lives at the intersection of Main and Hall of Fame. The surreal war zone I experienced at Main and Hall of Fame betrayed how I believed my world, my small town, is *supposed to* be. Just three hundred yards away, my little two-year-old boy was playing and laughing with his cousins, full of innocence, just how I believed the world of a two-year-old is supposed to be. However, where I stood, someone else's two-year-old boy had just tragically died. The world where my son was safe was no more. This is what suffering does, it betrays our trust in how the world is supposed to be. It betrays how *our* lives should be, and what we believe God's role is in protecting it all.

If you are living with a person active in addiction, it feels like a war zone. If you live with an abusive spouse, you are most definitely living in a war zone. If you have the type of boss who bulldozes and gaslights everyone in the office, you work in a war zone. There are no bullets flying or RPGs launching, no medevacs are circling or people screaming, but there is an intense traumatic betrayal of how you imagined your life playing out, either at home or the office.

Living with a person active in their addiction is traumatizing. To work for a tyrant is traumatizing. To watch your child endure chemo is crushing. Regardless of your suffering, your sense of peace is tormented. Your head is preoccupied with anxious thoughts. Maybe most days, like me, your adrenaline surges. Your anxiety paralyzes. You live in fear. Your nervous system is accosted and put on high alert for indefinite periods of time.

Your body is pumping out cortisol like crazy. Your senses are a wreck, hyper-sensitive to smell and sound. Your mind swirls with anxious thoughts, such as: *Is his speech slurred, or am being crazy? Why is he not picking up his phone? Is the cancer back? Is my marriage over? Is he cheating again? Will my son ever have anything to do with me again?*

This is where denial kicks in. We use denial as a coping mechanism or as a defense mechanism to keep us safe from having to face the hurt, the hurt that life as we know it has been drastically altered. And no one is exempt; no one is concealed from their life's dream one day, without notice, turning into complete carnage. And when it happens we hang onto our denial because we falsely believe it protects us from facing the hurt we know is out there. But it doesn't. In the end, pretending the hurt isn't there, we get hurt much more and it's not just psychological. We get hurt spiritually as well.

COUNT IT, THEN MAKE IT COUNT

Denial in the short run is not a bad thing. It helps us cope or maintain normalcy to function when a crisis arises. Denial is our knee-jerk defense against the pain that assaults our sense of peace. It is understandable, just not sustainable. When we believe we can sustain our denial for the long haul, it becomes destructive. When we refuse to accept the reality of the suffering we face, there comes a very real risk that in our desperate attempt to reestablish control we end up losing more control. The two drinks lead to hangovers and warnings at work. The comfort of instant gratification online one day leads to an all-out obsession and an empty, lonely, comfortable bed after your spouse has forgiven you for the last time.

What fuels our denial? At denial's core are survival and protection. We want to protect our peace of mind against the emerging dark clouds forming over the horizon of our comfortable lives. We want life as we know it to survive the inconvenience of tragedy. We don't want to believe the suffering we face will alter everything when it actually already has. We want our child, our marriage, or our career to survive. Denial isn't always outright blindness to the reality of a trial either, it can be partial as well. Often we can accept the reality that something is wrong, we just won't let ourselves believe that something is *too* wrong to actually do anything about it. But we must.

Denial, of course, is dangerous to both our body and mind, but denial is also dangerous spiritually. Our faith suffers when we don't have the courage to face the suffering we are dismissing. Maybe your life isn't shaking out the way you had planned. I don't know why you are reading this book. I don't know who you've lost or what dream of yours you feel is disappearing, but I do know denial is dangerous to us because it stunts our spiritual growth. God wants to radically alter you into looking like Jesus. Denial is spiritually sapping because it keeps our attention diverted away from what God is attempting to do for us through our suffering.

We get so hung up on our plans being interrupted and our convenience being inconvenienced that we miss the supernatural work God is calling us to accept. Denial keeps us from allowing God to radically alter us through our suffering. We want the suffering to end as soon as possible so we do everything to circumvent the very pain that God is planning to use to alter us into looking like His Son. Don't get me wrong, we want to do everything within our power to help relieve the suffering of those who are hurting. We also want to do anything we can to get help for ourselves if in crisis. However, when God is making it abundantly clear He is calling us into a season of suffering, we must suffer well.

James, the half-brother of Jesus, tells us to respond to our sufferings the opposite of our knee-jerk defense of denial. James tells us to count it all joy—to recognize the trial with joy—and keep on suffering until our faith matures to the point God desires. He writes for us not to deny it, but to count it. "Count it all joy, my brothers, when you meet trials of various kinds" (James 1:2 ESV). Something obvious James tells us is that believers will be met by various kinds of trials; and when we collide with these trials we are to count it all joy. To "count it" means to regard or consider it. Consider suffering as something to rejoice about?

This seems ridiculously impossible and it is unless you know something critical. James tells us if we are to count it all joy, we must know that suffering will produce spiritual maturity in us. What we all need to know in order to count it as joy is this: the testing of your faith produces endurance and afterward your faith is made mature. The NASB puts it this way, "knowing that the testing of your faith produces endurance. And let endurance have *its* perfect result, so that you may be perfect and complete, lacking in nothing." We can get to a place where we endure suffering with joy because we know the glorious outcome.

The Greek word here for *endurance* is a compound word that means "remain under." If we accept the reality that God has brought suffering into our life for an indefinite amount of time and then faithfully remain under the weight of it, God will grow our faith to make us spiritually mature. He alters us. These trials we fall into are the very catalyst by which God launches our faith onto a new sphere of spiritual maturity. Trials that test our faith stretch our faith. As our faith stretches and grows, it matures; we mature. We alter. We become like Jesus, who suffered in ways we can't imagine.

How do we pivot from desperately denying something to rejoicing in light of it? How do we count it all joy? How do we consider it all joy when *it* is so scary? First, for us to count it, we stop denying it. We accept it and welcome it, though we may hate it. Second, by no longer denying it we are free to then count it with all joy because we know it will mature us. It will make us more like Jesus. Third, after we count it, we make it count by remaining under the trial because we know God's plan is replacing our own broken plan and His plan is better than anything we could dream up on our own. We rejoice, not in the present suffering but in what God promises to do in the end through our present suffering. However, if we continue to deny it, not only will our denial keep us in the dark as to what God is doing, but it will also keep us from participating with God in our own transformation. We cannot faithfully endure a trial, and so be matured by it, if we fearfully refuse to believe it even exists in the first place.

Persistent denial is a spiritual disaster of the worst kind because it keeps us from being radically altered into the image of Jesus. If we want to be conformed more and more into the image of Jesus, who suffered on our behalf, then we mustn't be surprised if God uses suffering as a means to get us there. If we want the suffering to count for something, then by faith we make it count by enduring for as long as it takes, knowing that by the grace of God we will be changed. We will be transformed. We will be altered. Denial may make us feel safe or protect our sense of peace in the short run, but really denial robs us. It will not only rob us of becoming more like Jesus but also of the unforeseen joy we discover in the midst of becoming more like Jesus. We must accept God's high calling that comes to us through our suffering—a calling that will radically alter us and others for His glory.

So count it with all joy because you know through your suffering God is on the move to do great things in you and through you. Knowing this about God and your suffering fortifies your faith to remain under your suffering until it has had its perfect result. We cannot respond in faith to our suffering while living a lie of denial. Maturing in faith requires of us to be honest with ourselves and courageous to face whatever the hard, scary, and sad reality we feel is assaulting our peace. Don't deny it; count it, then make it count.

CHAPTER 3

You Can't Fix It

I RUSH HOME IN MY TYPICAL ANXIOUS, BUT HEROIC, FASHION. MY stomach tangled in a mess of knots. The menacing feeling that twists tightly inward claims me once more. As I drive home each anxious minute passes like the delayed tick of a dying clock. The nine minute drive always felt like a nine hundred mile journey. I knew things were not good with Heidi and I need to get home. She abruptly stopped communicating with me earlier. She had gone dark in our communication for over thirty minutes, which was always a sign she had been drinking. I finally arrive home. I walked into the kitchen through the garage. My kitchen looked like a crime scene. It looked like a slaying had taken place. A massacre of an epic proportion mixed with food on the floor and mingled in among the broken glass on the counter, all of which suggested that someone had suffered an egregious wound. My eyes moved to the sink where I saw a large knife that had been used recklessly. My eyes continue to move up to the right. I see paper towels strung out everywhere, but I don't see Heidi. The whole scene is vicious and vile as I feel a sense of panic rise in me. I call out to her, but nothing. I scan around the house and she is nowhere. I run to our bedroom to find her out cold on the bed with her hand wrapped in a wad of red, soggy, paper towels.

There was a small event that night of which Heidi had volunteered to provide the finger foods (pun definitely intended). I sifted through Heidi's texts and call log to see who she had been talking with and what she was responsible to bring. Once I figured out her responsibilities, I thought, *I can fix this!* Being a youth pastor and college pastor, I had become pretty skilled in the art of snacks and dips. I throw away all the contaminated food (because, you know, it had mixed in with the massacre) and I start making spinach dip and Heidi's famous "healthy queso." I cut all the veggies and arrange them on the circular platter. Celery. Carrots. Broccoli. You name it, I got it chopped and organized. Once assembled I ran the food out to the person setting up for the event that evening. I gave the lame excuse that I had become accustomed to giving, which was that Heidi had randomly come down with some virus. I assure this person that the food was all good and has not been contaminated by her germs. I had followed Heidi's directions from a safe distance. I lied. I fixed it. I saved her reputation and rescued the event. No one would be the wiser. I felt heroic in a weird way. I felt heroic in a sad way.

I may have fixed the gruesome mess, but I had not fixed the real mess: BPD. One of the hardest things to accept, especially if you are the parent of someone suffering from substance abuse or mental illness, is the fact that you can't fix it. You can do a lot to help, but you cannot fix it. You cannot protect them from it. You cannot cure them of it. If you believe you can heroically fix *this*, whatever *this* may be in your life, you are still in denial and will continue to practice fixing. And fixing doesn't fix the real mess. You certainly cannot fix whatever God is calling you to undergo. So if we can't fix it, what are we to do?

While Heidi was in rehab, I went to my first Al-Anon meeting. At this point, I thought it couldn't hurt. Al-Anon meetings, like AA, are a bit confusing if you've never been before. These meetings have their own slogans and mottoes. They tend to pick up where the meeting before left off, and not every meeting is the same. Some meetings are over the twelve steps and traditions. Some are "Big Book" studies. Some are topical. Some AA meetings are open, but most are closed. I didn't really know what I was doing.

We sat in a small circle, almost too big for the small church library lined with bookshelves. Around the room, the atmosphere held together with a sense of calm grief, happy hope, and a hint of inexpensive coffee. As we settled into our steel foldout chairs, we agreed on a topic from the index in the back of the book I was handed. We went around the circle, each person reading a short writing, much like a devotional, on the topic of detachment. After finishing the reading, the reader could briefly share if they felt like it. I felt stupidly nervous like I was back in fifth-grade reading class. As my turn approached, rounding the circle closer to me, the more like a child I grew nervous. My turn had finally arrived. I blew through my reading as fast as possible. As I was reading, I came across the word *ricochet* and said *ratchet*. I felt so dumb. After I read, I felt like I had to share something, but I had no idea what I just read. So not knowing what to say (I still don't know exactly what I said), I made a joke to mask my insecurity. After accepting a few polite laughs, I passed to the next reader.

I didn't know what I was expecting to find there. Some quick tips on how to fix Heidi perhaps. Maybe I thought Al-Anon was a bunch of people like me who sat around drinking coffee, sharing war stories, and secrets about how to fix each other's problems. They did have coffee, but no quick fixes.

One thing I took away once the hour meeting ended was one of their most commonly spoken slogans known as the Three Cs. *I didn't cause it, I can't control it, and I can't cure it.* I wasn't looking for catchy slogans; I was looking for a fix. Perhaps you're looking for a quick fix too, but there isn't one. There is nothing you can read, there is nothing you can learn, and there are no insider secrets or pro tips to circumvent the hurt God wants to use to grow you.

When we realize there are no quick fixes to our suffering, we should move on to acceptance. Most (like me), however, out of a desperate and misplaced hope to fix, continue to vainly reestablish control by modifying our efforts. I modified my efforts to fix Heidi's drinking by moving her to a different environment, even a different state. That didn't work, so I thought if I got her out of the tiny apartment and into her dream house, that would fix it. It did not. I thought that at the root of her problem was her infertility, so I took her to a specialist and got her knocked up. The baby didn't fix it. Everything positive I tried did not fix it. So, instead of fixing Heidi's behavior, I then contrived to control her behavior. This is where things really start to get messy.

HIDE-AND-SEEK

As I mentioned, the new environment in Oklahoma that I thought would fix Heidi's drinking didn't work. It actually turned out to make it worse. We were now in a small town where it was no longer kosher to drink at 3:00 p.m. on a patio somewhere for happy hour. Now she was a pastor's wife, so it wasn't really kosher for her to sit on a patio at any time to drink. This led to her shoe wine closet drinking. Can't go to happy hour? Make your own happy hour. After I found the shoe wine, I controlled her by taking her access to cash away, and I made sure she knew if she went to the liquor store with her debit card I'd see it on the bank statement immediately. Well, not immediately, but she didn't know. I thought for sure I had ended her shoe wine stashing and fixed her behavior by taking control of her. She proved me wrong.

One evening we were at my parents' house. Heidi needed to run to Walmart just down the street for something random. I thought it was strange but acquiesce none the less. She returned thirty minutes later. Within minutes of arriving, she went from normal Heidi to very chatty Heidi. I knew soon she would be completely altered, slurring her words, and losing control. I immediately say good-night and push her to the door. I did not know what she drank or how much, but I thought we needed to get her back to the apartment as soon as possible, which was just a mile away.

Like anyone in survival mode, you do dumb things that make no sense. I wanted to protect Heidi's reputation with my parents, so I told her to get in her car and get home while I followed in my car. I put protecting her reputation above protecting her life and others. This is the definition of fixing in the world of substance abuse. Everything took a backseat to fixing the reality of the situation, including safety and honesty.

We didn't make it far before I could tell her driving home wasn't going to work. I flash my lights at her to pull over, but she doesn't. I feel the rush of adrenaline and cortisol sweep through me, erasing any sense of calm I may have had left. As she drives on erratically there is no peace, no comfort, only that anxiety that strangles each breath. I speed up and cut her off, hoping she wouldn't slam into the back of me. She stops. I get out to help her toward my car. She slurs she's fine and can drive. As I help her navigate to the passenger seat, I notice a car parked in front of a house directly across from us. On the back window was our church's window sticker. *Great*, I thought unenthusiastically. I get her loaded, and we head home.

Once we are back at our apartment, I get Heidi tucked in bed. I then take off into the December night on foot. I don't run in the normal sense. I have a knee that doesn't bend. Heidi says when I run, it looks like I'm playing with the 1990s toy Skip-It, but the Skip-It is invisible. So there is the bum leg, then you add in the stifling cold and skin biting wind. Not fun. The whole run, my mind plagued, *What if that person with our church sticker saw me moving Heidi from her car into mine? What if it got out among the church? Worse, what if my boss found out?* Fixing the mess is all I could think about, and the only way to fix it was to get her car home as fast as possible.

After she sobered up, I asked how she did it. She denied doing anything of course, but I found a receipt. At first glance, there was nothing alcoholic there. Just random things like gum, beef jerky, and HH. *What is HH? She bought two. Where are they?* I do a little digging on walmart.com and Google to figure out that HH is Holland House cooking sherry. I look up to see if cooking sherry is like the sherry the eclectic Crane brothers drink in the sitcom *Frasier*. Close enough. It depends on what you buy, but there is roughly 17 percent alcohol in cooking sherry.

I had failed to fix her; I failed to control her behavior. She figured a way around my policing her bank statement. My denial, my inability to fix her behavior, and my bruised ego led me to ratchet up my controlling efforts. I tightened the chain I had around her. I took her debit card. She would snap out of it now for sure. She lost her cash and now debit card.

Some time had passed, not too much time but enough for me to drop my guard and for her cloaked borderline creativity to grow more cunning. I'm away and once more Heidi goes dark. She knows not to go dark on me, ignoring my texts and calls. I spin out. I rush home. I walk in the door and call out her name. There is no response. I know it has happened again. I look in the bedroom, but she is not there. She is not in the living room either. I go into another room and there she is, slumped in a chair out cold.

Similar occasions like this kept happening once or twice a week. For the life of me, I could not figure out how it was happening. Because I had become so hyper controlling, she had no cash. She wasn't allowed to carry or use her debit card without me. She only used it when I gave it to her at the store. I comb through every item on her receipts and nothing. And yet, somehow I keep finding empty cooking sherry bottles concealed throughout the house. I'm finding empty bottles in the closest. I'm finding bottles tucked away in a filing cabinet. But I cannot figure out how she's purchasing them.

I become obsessed with finding her method of buying and stashing. It becomes a weird, little, twisted game of hide-in-seek. I have to find the stash before she drinks it. If she drinks it, I lose. She wins. She would hide it and I had become obsessed with seeking and finding it.

One day as I'm on one of my typical hunting exhibitions

throughout our home, I come across two Walmart gift cards. This seemed strange so I look up the card balance and history on walmart.com. There it is. Holland House Cooking Sherry. I scored a major win. I arrogantly confront Heidi about the gift cards. I feel good as I take possession of the cards and sleep well that night. Then it happens again. And again. I soon realize I have no idea how she's getting these gift cards. After a long time, I find she is getting them as gifts. Other times, she would make returns and have the balance put on a gift card. With this knowledge, I take the next logical step. I take her car keys. I've fixed this. She can't get sherry if she can't get to the store.

More time passes as her impulsivity grows more desperate. It all flares up again. I arrive home to find her passed out. On some occasions, I would find her on the living room floor or bedroom floor. Sometimes on the couch or bed. Every time was equally terrifying. Every time equally crushing. The cycle starts over. She mysteriously drinks and with a ferocious stubbornness, I launch my hunting exhibition throughout the house. I can only hunt so much though; the house is bigger than the 805-square-foot apartment. More nooks and crannies to hide things; there are more rooms and closets to stash things. She's also become more advanced in her creativity of discovering these hiding places. With every mood altering episode, I retaliate with more rules and more policing. I requite with more control and more desperateness.

The more I controlled her, the more creative and cunning she became. The weird, little, twisted game escalated into a proverbial fistfight. She hit me by drinking, then I hit her back with more sanctions. The manipulation and attempts to control each other intensified as time went on and grew more out of control. I was not loving her; I was controlling her. I was not helping her; I was punishing her. The irony is that the more I controlled her behavior, the more out of control her behavior became. The more I took control of the situation, the more out of control the situation became. I was determined to corner her, lay siege to the monster within her until I had my wife back. But it doesn't work that way. Controlling her actually intensified the narcissistic tendencies of her overlooked BPD and caused her to adapt to get her fix, which robbed me of mine. In all of my hustling to fix things, I wasn't fixing the real mess. I was making it worse.

The adverse effect from my attempts to fix Heidi's behavior devolved to a new, dangerous, and devasting low. I was not finding sherry bottles anymore, but I was finding Heidi worse than ever. My hunts throughout the house for the source of her intoxication raged on with no success. I was stumped. I had no leads. There was not an ounce of evidence as to what she was doing. I searched drawers, boxes, cabinets, closets, trash cans, and the bank account. Nothing. As I searched, I kept moving aside empty bottles of hand sanitizer. I didn't think anything of it as I dug under papers and into the back of junk drawers.

One day, after finding an unusual amount of hand sanitizer bottles, I thought that maybe she was drinking the junk. Not really believing it—because that would be crazy—I looked it up. After a quick Google search, I discovered the sobering fact that people do drink it to get intoxicated. I read of a hospital removing their hand sanitizer because an elderly person in their care had consumed it. Heidi denied it. But then, after a bad day, I smelled her breath, and it confirmed the heart-crushing truth that she had now resorted to drinking hand sanitizer in response to our weird, little, twisted game, in which I cut off all her access to alcohol.

I didn't know what to do. I lived with the fear of her dying almost daily pressed up against my anger that she would do something so self-destructive. I cried for her when she was passed out and yelled at her when she was awake. There were countless evenings after six or seven, even eight hours, of her being unconscious it occurred to me she may never wake up. I can't count how many times on these horrible days I thought to myself, *I'll probably never see her again.* Would she have brain damage? After being unable to awaken her for six or seven hours, I would lie next to her in bed and hold her hand like the night I first caught hers in mine when she stepped into that hole. But these nights, as I monitored her breathing, she wouldn't hold mine.

When you are young and married, you sometimes stop and think about what your future will look like. You picture your future in a certain way. I tried not to picture a future caring for a brain-dead wife. I had to kick out of my head many times the scene of our girls' wedding days and telling them they looked beautiful and that their mom would be so proud. Or other big dates like graduations or sixteenth birthdays. What would I tell our son when he asks where his mommy went? A little boy looks up to his daddy, but he needs his mommy to kiss his scrapes and to cuddle him when he's sick. I had tightened my grip of control so hard around her, hoping it would fix her behavior, but the monster in her did what it had to do to get its fix. I know now I didn't cause it, I can't control it, and I can't cure it, but I did make it worse. I made it worse because I didn't understand the upside-down world into which I followed Heidi. I thought I could outsmart it. I thought I could control it. I thought I could fix it, but I could not. I thought I could fix her, but I cannot.

ENTRUST IT

We cannot fix whatever God is calling us to undergo. So if we can't fix it, what are we to do? We entrust it. Like we saw in the previous chapter when we encounter suffering of various kinds, our natural reaction is self-preservation. We deny it to buy us time. With this time we frantically attempt to fix it, whatever it may be. We try to end the pain as soon as possible because it's a threat to life as we know it. It assaults our sense of peace and comfort. Self-preservation is why we try with all we have to circumvent the pain or hurt. Controlling and fixing the problem is our vain attempt to do just that.

Suffering, however, has a way of reeling in our overconfidence back to the reality that we truly are not in control of our lives. "Tragedies rid us of the overconfidence we have that we are in control of our destinies."[3] Control is an illusion we all operate under to some degree. It is like a spell that bewitches us, and suffering, after some time, has a way of breaking that spell. While under the spell, we always set out naïvely believing we have the power to end the hurt. What we really should do is let the pain be the humbling antidote to break the spell of our omnipotence.

Once the spell is broken, we accept it and then we determine to endure it. We don't endure it by our feeble attempts to fix it. We endure the suffering by fully entrusting it. We entrust it to God. Then for the unforeseeable future, we live in this place of faith and utter dependence on God, while the suffering has its maturing effect on us. Only the extent to which we trust God can be the extent to which we endure. We might be able to take steps to improve our hurt or bring about a quicker conclusion, but many things we really can't fix quickly. We really can't fix most hurts we encounter or the real mess underneath driving it. Sure, we can paint makeup on it. We can slap a mask over it. We can stick a Band-Aid on it. But we can't fix what's going on beneath it. At least not quickly.

We can, however, learn to entrust it to God while we endure what He's calling us to face. You may need to entrust a situation with a coworker or boss. Perhaps you need to entrust a teenager or an aging parent. You may need to entrust yourself or a diagnosis to God. Maybe it's a lack of a diagnosis you must entrust to God like my parents had to do with me for a while when I was a child.

I understand it sounds very churchy to say that we should entrust it to God, but let me explain how I began working toward entrusting my situation to God. I would get up early in the morning because, honestly, I was terrified of what might be in store for me that day. Would I have to deal with the police that day? Would her drinking sabotage my college event that night?

During the time that I would get alone with God, I would tell myself over and over again that God created Heidi in His own image and He loved her. I told myself over and over God loved Heidi so much more than I ever could. He loved her so much that He sent His one and only Son to die a shameful and painful death on her behalf. Heidi had trusted in Jesus for eternal life and she belonged to God, not to me. He had purchased her by the blood of His own Son. Heidi was God's, not mine. I am not in control of her life. God is in control.

I prayed for myself as well. I prayed for God to help me give up just an inch at a time. I prayed He'd help me stop my anxious control of her. If Heidi wanted to get in the car and leave the house, I had to let her go. I had to let the fear of her potentially driving under the influence drive me to prayer and confidence that God had her. Every time this happened I asked for His strength. Some days I did well, and others I did not.

Every time I make the hard decision not to fix or police Heidi I'm entrusting her to God's control instead. It is not a one and done act. It is a daily act of faith. Really, it is more like a moment by moment act of faith. It is so hard to just stop and trust God when you're right in the middle of a situation that is so out of control. It is hard to have faith to lay down control when everything in you is screaming to take up control. Entrusting our suffering to God is a process of learning to lean on God's strength and not our own. It's the excruciating process of learning to loosen our grip on the things we so desperately want to control or we are too scared to let go. It's not easy and it takes a lot of strength. How do we, in our determination to endure our suffering, gain this strength to entrust it to God? We make it count when we first accept it, then endure it. We accept it knowing God has a good plan and we endure it knowing it is for our good. We can then entrust it, knowing God is fully able to bring His good plan and our good together because He's an infinitely good God. This all takes faith.

We, however, often make the mistake of treating faith like it is some sort of commodity. We say things like "If I only had more faith" or "I wish I had more faith." The key to entrusting our suffering to God isn't having more faith; it is having a maturing faith. Crucial to a maturing faith is knowing this truth: it is not the amount of faith but how well you know the object of your faith—Jesus. If we want to have a faith that continues to endure and mature during difficult times; a faith strong enough to entrust any situation, we must continue to increase in a robust relationship with Jesus, the object of our faith.

Jesus's disciples came to Him with the request of increasing their faith, and Jesus tells them that if they only had faith the size of a mustard seed, nothing would be impossible for them. They didn't need more faith; they needed a mature faith. They didn't need increased faith; they needed increased knowledge of the surpassing goodness of the character of their God. What you know about God will result in the strength to entrust your hurt to Him. If you believe God, who is the object of your faith, is more than capable to handle your crisis, then you will be strengthened to entrust your crisis to Him. If, however, what you believe about God is that He is unreliable and not always able to deliver, then your faith will prove immature and weak. You will have little strength from a little faith like that. Our faith rises to the level to that which we think of God. The higher and loftier we think of God, the stronger our faith grows to entrust, endure, and mature further.

For our faith to rise in maturity, we have to first have a high view of God. To gain such a lofty view of God, we have to pick up our Bibles. God gave us His word so we could know Him and live in His strength. If we think lowly of our God, our faith will strengthen us only to the shallow rocky depths its roots have reached. Then when the time of testing comes, we will give up on God because our faith had shallow roots. If you think lowly of God or have a shallow view of God, you will have a shallow faith. Paul tells his readers in Colossians 1:9–14 that he prays for them to be filled with the real knowledge of God's will in all spiritual understanding. This knowledge of God and His desires directly impacts the way we live for Him and our strength to entrust ourselves to Him, in order to endure. As we learn more about the glorious character of our God, the more we will entrust ourselves to Him. By this, we will be strengthened to persevere with patience and joy, while at the same time able to give thanks to Him. Increased knowledge of God and His will through the spiritual wisdom that we receive from God's word will lead us to live out a faith worthy of Jesus (Colossians 1:10).

As we come to this more robust understanding of who God is, this understanding which comes from our Bible, we are ushered into a strength to lean on Him with joy while we remain under our suffering. Our goal isn't to increase in faith; our goal is to increase in knowledge of who our God is and grow in our relationship with Him (Colossians 1:10). This increase in knowledge of God leads to a faith strengthened to withstand and endure; a faith becoming more and more mature. And the cycle continues: the more we mature through knowledge of Him the more we're strengthened to endure. The more we endure the more we mature because we see Him be true to who we've trusted Him to be in times suffering. Our aim is not to achieve more faith to face our seemingly insurmountable suffering, but growing a faith strengthened to entrust any situation, then endure it and be further matured by it. It's not the amount of faith we can muster up for God; it's about a mature faith placed in God.

Out from this mature faith and robust relationship with God, will emerge a newly shaped perspective of our suffering. This newly shaped perspective is the view that suffering isn't something to run from, but by faith courageously and joyfully face. Only when we have the courage of faith to face our hurt by hurling ourselves into the gracious hands of God, does He then begin the supernatural work of radically altering us into His Son's image. Only then, does He really begin to mold us into the image of the One who for the joy set before Him endured the cross scorning the shame (Hebrews 12:2). The joy set before Him was obeying the Father regardless of the intense shame He would endure. Jesus's view of His Father was so high that not even shame and death could obviate His obedience and joy. The same can be yours.

Verses like this in the Bible reveal to us the very character of God the Son, and it is His character, not our circumstances, that should influence our character in our suffering. He is our example. Jesus was able to entrust Himself to His Father during the most paramount act of evil against Him, and He could do so because He knew His Father well. He knew His character—righteous. "and while being reviled, He did not revile in return; while suffering, He uttered no threats, but kept entrusting *Himself* to Him who judges righteously" (1 Peter 2:23 NASB). He knew that although His suffering was unjust, He had a just Father whose plan was bigger than His present chaotic circumstances of the cross. He endured or remained under His painful circumstances for you and me, and He was strengthened to do so joyfully because He knew His Father better than anyone. That knowledge of His Father in all spiritual understanding of His will led to obedience to endure. Rather than focusing on His circumstances, Jesus allowed the joy that comes from a robust relationship with His supremely good Father to strengthen His ability to entrust Himself. For the joy set before Him (not His circumstances), Jesus was able to endure the cross.

Our faith weakens when we focus our attention away from God and onto our present circumstances as they seem to career into chaos. When we focus on our circumstances it is all too easy to believe that our God is not doing His job very well. We don't trust people who don't do their jobs well. If, however, we turn our attention to what God's word has taught us about His timeless character, our faith will rise to the strength of that truth and so strengthen us to entrust and endure, regardless of the ongoing storm of our chaotic circumstances.

By training ourselves to shift our attention away from our negative circumstances toward God's goodness found in His word, our minds are renewed. Neuroscience tells us that thinking certain thoughts over and over, day after day strengthens pathways in our brains. As we increase in knowledge of God and think of Him in a new way—a loftier way—we strengthen new pathways about Him. Day after day of thinking highly and rightly about God, your brain begins to change. Your brain begins to transform. You begin to transform. Focusing on repeating spiritual truths about God's love and unrelenting character to yourself each day, you make them second nature to your thought life. You make God's truths and promises automatic thinking. This is huge because your thoughts determine how you live. They will steer your steps. "For as he thinks within himself, so he is" (Proverbs 23:7 NASB).

You cannot control or fix it. You certainly cannot control or fix other people's behavior as I attempted with Heidi, but you can control your own behavior, which begins with your thoughts. You can't control what the world and others hurl at you, but you can control how you will respond. That response will largely be a result of how well you know God—how high you view God. If you train your brain to automatically default to lofty truths such as "God is with me. God is fighting for me. God loves my loved one more than I can imagine," you will respond in a spiritually transformed way to your crisis.

However, if you continue to allow your thoughts to default to negative pervasive thinking, such as *My life is so miserable. God never gives me a break. I can't do this anymore. I hate God for this! I hate my job. I hate my body,* then you will not be radically altered into looking like Jesus. We must entrust it and ourselves to God, who is a righteous judge, just like Jesus obediently entrusted Himself to God because He knew God would make all the right calls.

"Fixing" doesn't fix the real mess, so stop trying to fix it. Instead, entrust it to God by fixing your eyes on Jesus, who has showed us how to entrust ourselves to the One who will handle us justly and rightly. We can't control our circumstances, but we can increase in knowledge of our God and in doing so see our faith strengthened to endure the most egregious of circumstances. If we do just this, focus on increasing in the knowledge of God, the result will be a mature faith and a supernatural strength to continue to endure, becoming even more spiritually mature. If, on the other hand, we do not increase in knowledge of our God, then any chances of enduring faithfully and becoming radically altered by Him, through our suffering, will diminish. God never gave us a quick way to fix it; He gave us the example of His Son, Jesus, to entrust it.

CHAPTER 4

Prefrontal Cortex Vortex

WHAT WAS HAPPENING TO THE TIE-DYED-T-SHIRT-WEARING, SUN-is-always-shining, glass-half-full-even-when-it's-almost-gone girl? Her enthusiasm was gone. She spent much of her time isolated in bed. Heidi was an extremely intelligent girl, but now she was doing something so unintelligent as drinking hand sanitizer. It didn't make sense. It's not as if as a little girl growing up Heidi had dreams of one day sneaking around consuming something as crude as hand sanitizer. Your son or daughter, while playing in the backyard, was not pretending to be an alcoholic or drug addict. They were not hiding up in the tree house pretending to shoot up with a Doc McStuffins syringe. They were pretending to be superheroes, playing house, baking mud pies, and playing in the sprinkler. Heidi was just like any other little child. She was just like you and me. But now she was a shell drained of all the fun and life I fell in love with and married years earlier. She was there physically, but behind her once optimistic brown eyes, she was being altered into someone else.

How insidious is a suffering that causes a person to lose them self; to live unable to remember who they are and what they value. Heidi would drink and drive. She would drink and go to church. Even when she wasn't drinking, she was acting out of control, saying things that would hurt people or betray other's trust. It did not matter how many conversations I had with her, she would not stop. I now know she could not stop. I was constantly on edge, wondering when the next phone call would come about something Heidi said or did. I would find excuses to cancel or not commit to anything social because I never knew which Heidi would show. Those things that I could not cancel caused me a great deal of anxiety. I dreaded going to work due to the impromptu meetings with my boss because Heidi said something to someone and caused problems for him in the church. It added a whole other layer of stress to my life which was already under duress. This wasn't Heidi anymore. It seemed every time she would say or do something, she did so without any forethought.

Now we know that most likely Heidi was acting without her forethought. The prefrontal cortex (situated above our eyebrows in the forefront of our head) is the smart part of our brain which executes judgment and impulse control. As Heidi settled into using alcohol as her main form of managing her unmanageable emotions brought on by her then untreated BPD, her brain began to rewire impulsive behaviors that resulted in more unmanageable emotions. The unmanageable emotions of shame, self-loathing, and a vacant worthiness were also rewired into crucial beliefs about herself. As a result, her thought life and self-image morphed into something diabolical: the belief she is unworthy of love and belonging.

Along with decreased activity seen in the prefrontal cortex in substance abuse, there is also seen a decrease in prefrontal activity observed in the brain of the borderline.

> Changes in brain metabolism and morphology (or structure) are also associated with BPD. Borderline patients express hyperactivity in the part of the brain associated with emotionality and impulsivity (limbic areas), and decreased activity in the section that controls rational thought and regulation of emotions (the prefrontal cortex).[4]

A change in brain structure might explain what was going on in Heidi, but why does it matter to you? If you are not a substance abuser or struggle with a personality disorder, what good is knowing your brain changes? The importance of this was so eloquently put by the beloved Dr. Seuss, "You have brains in your head. You have feet in your shoes. You can steer yourself in any direction you choose."[5] You have a brain and what you choose to do with it—the thoughts you choose to think about yourself, God, and others—directly affect your emotions and actions. Your thoughts are important because the thoughts you allow will determine the direction they will steer you.

My son and I went on an "adventure" around the pond behind my parents' home. There is a wooded area that is separated from the pond by a levee. We all call it the dam. As children, we neighborhood kids would play in those woods. We built forts, climbed trees, and got poison ivy in those woods. Starting on top of the dam, we made a bike trail going down the wooded hill extending through the trees and coming out in a clearing below to the left. This trail doubled as an awesome sledding track the few years we got a good snow.

As my son and I walked along the dam that day between the tree line and pond, I pointed to where I used to ride my bike down. The once clearly defined trail, however, was gone. After years of not being used, the grass and weeds had overgrown the trail. There were even small trees that had grown up where the Oklahoma hardpan trail once descended, quickly zigzagging through the trees. It had grown up so much that I wasn't even certain where I was pointing was in fact the old entrance.

Our brain is made up of close to 100 billion neurons. These neurons connect, creating networks or neural pathways throughout our brain. These pathways in our brain are traveled every time we think a certain thought, feel a certain emotion, and act a certain way. The more we use these pathways, like the bike trail, the more clearly defined and worn they become. As these pathways become deepened and strengthened by our repeated thoughts, feelings, and actions, they become automatic to us or second nature. When we stop traveling these neural pathways and make new ones by changing how we think, it changes how we feel and, subsequently, how we act. As we travel these new pathways, the old ones over time weaken and become overgrown. These weakened or "overgrown" pathways are not easily found and traveled anymore, like my old childhood bike trail.

Just as neural pathways weaken and become overgrown with less use, pathways traveled more frequently by our thoughts, feelings, and actions strengthen and deepen. The brain changes because of what's called neuroplasticity. Our brains are plastic. They are malleable. They change. They are altered by our thoughts and actions. And so we are altered by them.

Suffering has a strong way of bringing out negative thoughts and ruminating resentments. These negative thoughts often form a vortex in our life that hurt us and those who are closest to us. These vortexes form when you and I respond with a poor thought life to our suffering. If we are to destroy these vortexes we must learn to capture these rogue thoughts before they entrench in our neural pathways and cause unimaginable grief to us and all who may get sucked in.

Dr. Caroline Leaf stresses this very importance in her book *Switch on Your Bain*. She writes, "When you objectively observe your own thinking with the view to capturing rogue thoughts, you in effect direct your attention to stop the negative impact and rewire healthy new circuits into your brain."[6]

The thoughts we choose to think about ourselves and the truths about God we hold onto while suffering, are crucial for who we are becoming. The pathways we have allowed our thoughts to travel will influence strongly how we will respond to our suffering. That response will affect who we will become. We can't choose what suffering comes upon us but we can choose, by the thoughts we allow, who we will be once the suffering has left us.

We know that spiritual transformation comes from the renewing of our thoughts according to God's word. Suffering has a profound way of breaking our thought life out of its routine, giving a greater focus to our suffering. So we focus a lot of our attention and internal monologue on our suffering during these times of pain. What we do with this focused attention is crucial for our becoming like Jesus. This is why Paul Tripp argues that suffering is spiritual warfare fought in the heart.[7] The thoughts, both positive and negative, we allow about ourselves and God while we suffer will directly affect how suffering will alter us, for better or worse. The pathways we choose to strengthen according to God's word will result in our ability to respond with joyful endurance, which will ultimately bring about us being altered into the image of Jesus. First, though, we must think rightly about ourselves and highly of Him, leaving behind any shallow thinking to be "overgrown."

THE VORTEX

The neural pathways running back and forth from Heidi's prefrontal cortex were being less traveled while most of the traffic in her brain was on a single path from her midbrain to her accumbens and probably up to her dorsal striatum. The more her BPD traits intensified, coalescing with the alcohol abuse, the stronger her impulsivity, lack of judgment, and inability to comprehend consequences grew. As these two coalesced more frequently, she began accessing less and less the part of her brain that thinks, *Stop.* Heidi was beginning to run on *Go, Go, Go,* and all of us close to her began getting hurt.

None of us can live on *Go*; we can't live based on pure desire and not hurt others and ourselves. This is why God has given us all a conscience, and for believers the added Holy Spirit, so we do not do the things we selfishly desire (Galatians 5:17). As the overwhelming thoughts and feelings of shame intensified, so did the self-destructive behavior to either relieve the existential pain inside her or at other times punish her for not being who she believed she was supposed to be. The intense shame Heidi feels at times is the overwhelming feeling of not being enough or feeling less than. Expert in the study of shame, Brené Brown, says this about it: "Shame is the intensely painful feeling or experience of believing that we are flawed and therefore unworthy of love and belonging."[8]

Shoe wine had become the blood that had to be poured out to expiate Heidi's own failings. And for a person suffering BPD that atonement has to be on hand at a moment's notice.

As I increased control over the access to her alcoholic absolution, it forced Heidi to find new and easier ways to escape the overwhelming feelings of being unworthy of love and belonging. Hand sanitizer became that new and easy escape. It had also become the new expiative elixir, both an escape and expiation that is virtually everywhere and impossible for me to control.

If it is the case in those who have borderline personality disorder, as well as substance abusers, that the pathways from the prefrontal cortex have weakened, and in some cases disconnected from the striatum, then it is not hard to see how Heidi got so out of control and her behavior so self-destructive. It most definitely could be argued that Heidi's prefrontal cortex had disengaged to some degree or lost efficiency as seen in her inability to function socially in some places without running to the nearest form of escape. Heidi's lack of ability to interpret her relationships and social settings due to the decreased activity of her prefrontal cortex created what I call the prefrontal cortex vortex, and everyone who got too close to her got sucked in and hurt.

The lie that she's not enough or less than entrenched itself so deeply in Heidi's thought life it became the driving force behind her substance abuse. This, most likely, originated back at those happy hours when Heidi saw herself as an unimportant temp in a big city of very important people. Happy hour had become Heidi's first shield to protect her from her delusional fear that people may find out that she was a "fraud" as she inwardly and incorrectly believed. Over the years as the diabolical lie *I'm unworthy of love and belonging* entrenched itself in her thought life, becoming a part of how she perceived herself, the shame grew more intense. As the shame swirled stronger within Heidi, the vortex outwardly surged uncontrollably, hurting those closest to her.

Heidi did not respond to her shame with God's truth about herself. Truths such as, she is enough, that she is already accepted by God as His daughter, and that she has tremendous value and worth not based on what others say, but on what God has already said about her. Instead, she responded poorly to the avalanching shame by attempting to alter herself into who she thought she was *supposed* to be, rather than taking God at His word for who she already was.

Since Heidi believed she wasn't worthy of belonging she drank thinking it would then alter her into someone fun people would want to be around, but the lie betrayed her and resulted in her feeling more rejected and ostracized. Ironically, in the end, her attempts to alleviate the shame caused her to feel the shame more intensely. After a while, her impulsivity to drink anything near her became her only means of escaping the unbearable shame and rejection she felt swirling within, leaving her feeling more and more empty. Jerold Kreisman and Hal Straus put it this way in their best-selling classic, *I Hate You—Don't Leave Me: Understanding the Borderline Personality*:

> Chronic emptiness depletes him until he is forced to do anything to escape. In the grip of these lows, the borderline is prone to a myriad of impulsive, self-destructive acts—drugs and

alcohol binges, eating marathons, anorexic fasts, bulimic purges, gambling forays, shopping sprees, sexual promiscuity, and self-mutilation. He may attempt suicide, often not with the intent to die but to feel *something*, to confirm he is alive.[9]

Instead of being met with unrelenting grace and chronic love, those of us feeling the intense pull of Heidi's prefrontal cortex vortex pushed back with harsh criticism and scathing contempt. Her shame beget drinking and her drinking beget shame, and around and around she goes. The more laps around, the more her negative thinking is reinforced. Her synapses strengthened and tightened. The more her negative self-ruminating is reinforced, the more her drinking becomes an automatic response to escape the internal pain, self-hate, emptiness, and loneliness she felt. Since alcohol is highly rewarding, neurologically speaking, it accelerated the rewiring of her limbic response (her shame/drinking cycle), disengaging her prefrontal cortex further. The result: she (as well as everyone close to her) fell victim to the prefrontal cortex vortex that emerged.

Volatile emotions such as shame influence all of our behaviors to a degree. Some to a higher degree than others, but most don't even realize it. In borderlines, the volatile emotions are much more intense and harder for them to manage, but we all battle shame. Regardless, how we choose to think about ourselves matters. Like Heidi, if we allow a negative thought life toward ourselves to entrench, a vortex will ensue. What we choose to believe about ourselves is crucial, especially in times of suffering. Knowing shame is something we all carry and affects our self-perception, especially in times of suffering, is helpful. Shame is a lie that perhaps a parent told us about ourselves when we were young, innocently we took hold of it, believing it our whole life. Shame could be a lie your spouse started telling you only a year ago about yourself, but for whatever reason, you latched on and have believed it ever since. Shame is even a lie our culture tells us and we accept as true without question.

Just think about beauty. What is beauty? Do you have a definition or idea of beauty that is different from the woman on the magazine cover or in the commercial? Now if you are a female, do you measure up to that idea of beauty? If you don't measure up, culture's definition of beauty leaves you feeling less than. Men, culture tells us what it means to be a man. Money. Big house. Nice vacations. Being amazing at sex. How do you measure up? If you don't, then you too feel less than. You feel shame.

In her book, *I Thought It Was Just Me (But It Isn't)*, Brown quotes Dr. Robin Smith on what shame does to us. "I will define who you are and then I'll make you believe that's your own definition."[10] We hear the lie day after day of who we are *supposed to* be and chase after it. For many, we negatively ruminate on a specific lie, day after day, completely dissatisfied in life because we can't catch it. We don't measure up to who we think we're *supposed to* be or have what we're *supposed to* have.

The more the lie becomes an entrenched part of our thought life, the more it shapes our identity and self-perception, as well as our perspective of the world around us. The self-perceptions we carry around of ourselves can be called a "supposed to," such as I'm *supposed to* be thin. I'm *supposed to* be making more money. I'm *supposed to* have a baby. When we fall short of the *supposed to* we (or someone else) has constructed for our life, we feel shame, and that shame left unchecked drives our attempts to escape the unsettling feelings it brings.

Look no further than Genesis 2 to see that we were not created to feel shame. In the beginning, we find Adam and Eve naked and unashamed. So when we feel shame, it cuts against the very fabric of who we are meant to be as image bearers of God. So naturally, when we feel shame, we do whatever we have to do to escape it, hide from it, or distract others away from it. Who we are truly *supposed to* be are men and women who feel no shame, no inadequacy, no vacancy of worthiness, and who enjoy a full sense of belonging.

Since Genesis 3, after Adam and Eve took the bait and believed the lie about God and themselves, God has been at work to bring men and women back to Himself through His Son, Jesus. This is reconciliation. Reconciliation isn't just the story of God restoring the relationship between us and Him only; He wants to restore you back with yourself. Through His Son, Jesus, He has been working to bring us back, not only to Himself but back to our self, to the true sense of knowing who we are in Him and our value—our true identity. We are meant to know our complete value and full significance before God. We are to know we are wholly loved and our acceptance by God is absolute—not because of anything we've done for God, but because of everything Jesus has done for us. And He uses suffering to do this.

Maybe you are responding to the suffering of your shame through mood-altering substances. Perhaps you are externalizing the hurt by blaming others. Suffering has a profound way of exposing what is hidden or overlooked in our hearts—our *supposed to* that is ever so elusive to catch. The more we entrench poor thinking toward our self, God, and others, the more we work against suffering's illuminating work in us. With a negative thought life about ourselves, we will be less likely to endure and more likely to respond poorly to our suffering, creating our own vortexes, which will only bring more harm to our hurt.

We have seen how poor thinking towards ourselves can produce vortexes in our lives, but poor thinking towards God is just as disastrous when it comes to our transformation. How we view ourselves is important but how high or low we see God is critical. The truths we receive and believe about God is paramount to our faith's ability to endure what God is calling us to face.

Jesus tells a famous parable about the ground. A man goes out to sow some seeds. Some seeds land on the ground, which is hard, and the seed can never germinate. It never had a chance because the ground was unable to receive the seed due to its hardness. Other seeds land in rocky soil. The seed germinates and grows up but dries out because the roots received no moisture. Still, other seeds fell on the ground among thorns, which eventually choked out the plant produced by the seed. Lastly, some seeds fell among the good soil and not only grew up, but produced a crop a hundred times as great.

The rocky ground, Jesus explains, are those who hear and receive the word with joy. However, because they have a shallow soil, their faith has shallow roots. So when it sprang up and the heat advanced against it, it dried out. Their shallow faith couldn't take the heat of life. Their faith has no firm root so they believe for a little while; they joyfully believe when all is well, but when things get tough, they fall away.

The roots of our faith will only reach as far as the depths of our understanding of God. If we have a shallow view of who God is, we will have a shallow faith in Him. The risk is that when the time of testing advances against us, our faith will dry out and we may rebel, revolt, or even desert the one we once joyfully celebrated for saving us.

The failure of this specific soil was not only that it was shallow but that it received rocks along with the seed. We all need to seriously consider what we are receiving; what are we believing as true about God that may actually not be biblical at all? Those very rocks worked against the faith's ability to mature its roots by reaching down deep to receive life-sustaining moisture. Is what we believe about God and how He works true, especially in suffering? Maybe some of these "truths" we've come to believe are actually rocks that will work against our faith from maturing in times of suffering. What "rocks" or lies about God are keeping your faith's roots from growing down deep?

Some rocks or lies that we receive about God are the following:

- God's job is to protect me from all harm because He loves me. After all, I am His child.
- God is required to grant me my prayers if asked with enough faith.
- God is punishing me.
- God has abandoned me.
- God is singling me out because of my sin.
- I've failed God, and He is disappointed in me.
- My health and wealth are based on how much faith I have or how much money I can give to God.

When suffering arises and lies such as these don't harmonize with what God is doing or allowing, confusion follows. For many, a crisis of faith follows. We try to harmonize how we think God should be acting with the lack of action we may actually be seeing. When suffering comes and shakes our belief about who God is and how He relates to us, our internal monologue goes into overdrive trying to rationalize our lies about God with our circumstances. The longer we hold to these lies, the easier a vortex can form. Over time, these lies produce a swirling flow of resentment, envy, anger, and blame within us. As the flow of these thoughts and emotions begin to surge a vortex of hate, drinking, cheating, and a dubious doubt of God's goodness form outwardly. And sadly, in intense times of pain, we see even some believers desert God altogether.

The greatest lie, and perhaps the most dangerous that we can slide into believing, is that God exists for our happiness. This myth will no doubt lead a person to abandon God when times of intense suffering come and we are hard pressed to find happiness. Does God want us to be happy? Absolutely. Is this the chief goal of God's existence? No. God wants us to be happy, but God does not exist for us or our happiness. His role in the universe is not to sit on His throne as our personal celestial genie servant. The happiness God wants for us is in a Christ-centered happiness found in Him.

There is a difference between enjoying a self-centered happiness and a Christ-centered happiness. Christ-centered happiness is found in surrender, whereas self-centered happiness is found in our stubborn attempt to achieve and maintain our own sense of comfort and peace on our own terms. In his book *Does God Want Us to Be Happy?* Randy Alcorn argues that God is a happy God and the source of our Christ-centered happiness. He takes on the notion circulated in Christianity that God wants us to be holy, not happy. Alcorn writes,

> To be holy is to see God as he is and to become like him, covered in Christ's righteousness. And since God's nature is to be happy (as we saw in chapter 2), the more like him we become in our sanctification, the happier we will be.[11]

Does God want us to be happy? Yes. However, God does not exist for this reason. He exists for His glory, and so do we. God wants us to find happiness in no other place than in fully following Jesus, and sometimes following Jesus takes us to places we don't want to go. But with Jesus as our source for happiness, and a very real presence in those places we don't want to go, we can enjoy happiness still while suffering there.

The truth that God is a happy God who wants us to be happy leads many to the sly idea that God must then exists for our happiness on our terms. This lie is faith crushing. In my late teens this lie almost crushed my faith.

I put my faith in Jesus at the age of nine. I had eternal life and knew I had eternal life. I, however, did not understand at the time the importance of being discipled. Without knowing it, I grew up with a shallow faith. I received the lie somewhere along the way that God would scratch my back if I scratched His. I saw my relationship with God as a quid pro quo type of relationship. I do good, and I get blessed. I do bad, and no blessings.

Blessings, also, were defined as simply what I want; things that fed into my self-centered happiness. In my mid to late teenage years, I encountered intense physical suffering with surgical procedures, which resulted in a lot of disappointment not being able to play competitive golf any longer. And then, to top it all off, my girlfriend dumped me for the captain of the football team. Unrequited love stinks.

So as the physical and emotional pain took its toll, my shallow faith led me to believe God was failing at His job. God was not living up to His end of the bargain because while in the midst of all my suffering, I was still going to church. I was staying away from the "big sins." I was even going to Wednesday night youth group! I prayed as I fell asleep in bed. I read my Bible for like a total of five minutes before spacing out and daydreaming for the next twenty-five minutes. I was doing my part, but God, for some reason, was holding out on me. He was keeping my happiness from me. I was miserable. I was mad. I was bitter toward God. The more I thought He owed me for my good works, the more miserable and bitter I became. And so, a vortex formed within me.

As a result of my shallow understanding of God and how our relationship worked, I arrived to the point where I couldn't believe God existed any longer. Since He wasn't playing by the rules, then He must not be there. I remember right where my mom was standing, in front of the kitchen sink, when I sent shock waves through her as I told her I wasn't sure God was real.

Before I committed to renouncing my faith, I thought I'd hate to get it wrong so I told God I would pour everything I had into seeking Him. I sat and read my Bible for hours some nights. I prayed longer. I went to every Bible study I could. I even wormed my way into my sister's college Bible study. I gave it my full attention so in case I got it wrong and stood before God, I could say, "I looked for You with everything I had, and You didn't care."

Over the course of doing these things with all I had, I started changing. My circumstances were still the same, but I wasn't. I have a distinct memory of sitting on the edge of my bed, looking at my Bible on the desk next to me thinking, *If you keep this up, you will turn into one of those lame goodie-good Christians.* The next thought was, *If I feel this alive, I don't care.*

Before I knew it, I was reading my Bible until 2:00 a.m. most mornings. I couldn't stop. The boring book had come alive, and I wanted to know more. I wanted to know more about Jesus. He went from just a Savior that I believed was real but distant to a Savior who was a masterful teacher and (I feel sarcastic) debater. He wasn't passive, and yet He never came off as the aggressor or instigator. He was just there doing His thing, not afraid of intense confrontation. The Pharisees never stood a chance against Him. Jesus was awesome. I wanted to be like Him for the first time in my life.

My shallow view of God and how our relationship worked was wrong and resulted in my spiteful bitterness toward God and envy toward others. It resulted in a vortex in my life. I was playing by an entirely different set of rules, which God wasn't, based on my good works. Our relationship with God is based on grace, not works. When it hit me I had the one thing I could ask God for—eternal life—and He gave it to me for free, I was crushed I had been so demanding in our relationship. If anything, He should have been the demanding one. He gave His Son, He gave me the unconditional gift of life, and I was a brat who wanted more. More golf trophies, the girl, whatever I wanted.

Having a works based relationship with God, especially in times of suffering, often leads us to resent God, because He blesses others we feel are less deserving. We then become envious of those less deserving because we tell ourselves they have those blessings which are *supposed to* be ours. Bitterness toward God, envy toward others, and around the vortex goes. It's a cycle. Our bitterness toward God grows stronger as we continue to believe He's not giving us what we believe He owes us. As our bitterness toward God strengthens, so does our envy toward others. When whatever it is we believe we deserve from God (often happiness or relief from suffering) doesn't come at our demand we start believing God is holding out on us; He is holding out on giving us what is supposed to be ours, our earned happiness.

When we don't respond in our suffering with God's truth about ourselves and Him, vortexes will form. For some, the vortex has already formed, causing more hurt for you and those around you. Maybe a vortex has already formed outwardly in your life; it has caused all kinds of destruction to you and harm to those around you being pulled in. If so, there is still hope. Regardless of how poor your thought life has been up to this moment, the good news is there is a way to destroy the vortex. There is a way to attack and dissipate the vortex that forms out of a swirling thought life in our suffering

VORTEX DESTROYER

A few years back, Heidi and I disembarked a plane by staircase down to the airport tarmac. As we walked up to the airport terminal, I noticed on the ground, around the front of the jet engine, a big semicircle of bright yellow paint. It was visibly clear by the markings that if you cross that line, you'd be sucked into the plane engine. There's no coming back from that.

Jet engines produce an enormous amount of force. As

the blade turns, it sucks air in through its intake. These jet engines generate such a force that as air travels into the air inlet, sometimes a vortex can form between the ground and the engine. This is problematic because if anything is on the ground near the vortex, it will be sucked right into the engine, causing damage to itself. Vortexes have sucked up off the ground things from screws to airline food carts, and even people. This is why vortexes are so dangerous, not only to the engine itself but to those who get too close.

The same is true when a vortex forms in our life out of the negative thinking that flows through our minds towards our self, God, and others. To allow these thoughts to flow unchecked will cause not only damage to us, but also to others who get too close. The good news is there is a solution: the vortex destroyer. Attached to the bottom front of some jet engines are vortex dissipaters. A vortex dissipater shoots a jet stream of air downward toward the ground where a vortex would form. This jet stream of air disrupts the air flow forming the vortex between the ground and the engine intake. This is how you destroy a vortex—you disrupt its flow.

We want to do the same thing to the vortexes that may form out of our thought life. Tripp wrote that in suffering, we trouble our trouble.[12] When we respond poorly to our suffering, we cause more grief and pain for ourselves and others. We have enough trouble so we don't want to create more trouble on top of our trouble by responding with a poor view of God. This is why we want to attack directly where the vortex will form before it happens.

The vortexes that form in our life always originate out from the same place, a poor thought life that drives a lifestyle outside of God's truth. A lifestyle that will eventually produce a surging vortex that sucks in others who get too close (Galatians 6:7–8). We want to attack and disrupt the flow of negative thoughts about ourselves, God, and others. This is crucial because what we think of as true about ourselves, the character of God, and those who are created in His image, will determine how we respond to the pain we feel inside and out.

The precarious belief that God is withholding happiness from us would truly discourage anyone. How is God good if He's not providing my happiness I feel is owed? If the discouragement persists, it turns to bitterness and loss of hope and faith. If we believe God is no longer good, we will certainly lose all hope. There is no hope in a God who is solely harmful. "Satan lies about himself, making himself to appear harmless. Then he lies about God, making God appear harmful."[13]

What good God would withhold happiness from His children? We falsely assume if life isn't good, then God isn't good, and if God isn't good, He must not be there. When we, with a shallow faith, hold onto the lie that God exists for our happiness, God will no longer appear good in times of suffering. He can't. As we allow the belief that God is not good to enter our thought life, it is only a matter of time before it entrenches and we desert the One who loves us so much that He delivered His own Son for us.

God is good, and our circumstances are not the measure of His goodness. If our circumstances are less than what we believe a good God should provide, we mustn't assume He is not there or not good, but know He has a good and loving reason. Make no mistake: God occupies Himself for our good, not always for making our circumstances good. God does not exist for our happiness; we exist for His glory, and He works for our ultimate good: being altered into the image of His Son. Your suffering isn't a sign God is not good, it is a sign that God is working for your good; to make you look more like Jesus whose life was marked by suffering.

We must push back against this lie that God exists to serve us. We have to disrupt the flow of such a thought, and suffering can be an opportunity to accomplish this. "We may imagine God as our genie who comes to do our bidding. Suffering wakes us up to the fact that we serve him, not he us."[14] We challenge this lie by allowing our suffering to shatter our present paradigm, to allow our suffering to drive our thinking of Him high above the idea of the genie servant to the realization that He is God and we serve Him. C.S. Lewis wrote in *A Grief Observed* that our idea of God is not a divine one, which God Himself shatters time after time. After God uses suffering to shatter our faulty idea of Him, not only do we see God truly but seeing Him alters our motivation into fully existing for Him.

In his letter to the Romans, Paul makes a major pivot, explaining that in view of the mercies God has already given them, they should sacrifice their selfish ways and live for Him. Paul did this by calling them to be living sacrifices for God. We don't sacrifice our selfish wants and desires only to then selfishly demand God now owe us our happiness. We do not leverage our good works for God, against God as a ransom, forcing Him to pay us back with happiness. He is not in debt to us in the least.

On the contrary, we should be in debt to Him for all He has done for us. We live a sacrificial life for Him because we know Jesus sacrificed His life so we could freely have new life in Him. So we stop letting the world with its lies and lusts conform us and mold us, and we start transforming by the renewing of our minds. We disrupt the thought flow of lies that form vortexes in our lives by shooting a jet stream of God's truth into our thought life.

These truths found in God's word, appraised by the Spirit, alter our thinking. They disrupt the flow of disobedient thoughts and allow you to take them captive as Paul did with his own thought life (2 Corinthians 10:5). We make new spiritual pathways in our brains that will alter us spiritually. We become radically altered by the Holy Spirit's power to change our thoughts to God's thoughts and our hearts to God's heart.

In our suffering, to become radically altered, we have to have radical thinking—otherworldly thinking—according to Paul, who writes, "Set your mind on the things above, not on the things that are on earth" (Colossians 3:2 NASB). Paul then goes on in verse 5 to tell his readers to use their otherworldly thinking to "consider the members of your earthly body as dead to immorality, impurity, passion, evil desire, and greed, which amounts to idolatry."

In Ephesians 4, Paul tells his readers to stop living like unbelievers who live "in the futility of their mind, being darkened in their understanding, excluded from the life of God because of the ignorance that is in them, because of the hardness of their heart" (Ephesians 4:17–18 NASB). In verses 22–24 he writes,

> that, in reference to your former manner of life, you lay aside the old self, which is being corrupted in accordance with the lusts of deceit, and that you be renewed in the spirit of your mind, and put on the new self, which in *the likeness of* God has been created in righteousness and holiness of the truth.

How we think of God, others, and ourselves will greatly determine how we live toward God, others, and our self. The more radical and otherworldly our thought life is, the more otherworldly our response will be in our suffering. We can destroy the vortex that forms out of our suffering by continually shooting a jet stream of God's truth about Himself and His goodness into our thought life. By this, we will disrupt the entrenched flow of negative thoughts about ourselves and lies we've been misled to believe about God.

Maybe you are struggling to believe God is good in light of the lack of good you see in your life. Maybe it feels as though God is withholding your happiness from you even now. Even if God is withholding your happiness from you (and He is not), He will never withhold His good from you. Remember this: God did not even withhold His own Son from you. He gave His one and only Son over to death for you when you could do nothing for yourself to get right with Him. He handed Jesus over to a brutal butchering, not for your self-centered happiness but for your good—to give you a new life that looks like His. God is not a God who withholds good from His children. He does the exact opposite, seen fully in the act of refusing to not withhold His very own Son. The strongest jet stream of truth we can fire to destroy the vortexes forming out of our thought life during times of suffering is the truth that God loves us so much that He didn't even withhold His one and only Son from us. A God who loves us like that cannot be out to harm us. Since God's goodness is seen in the act of not withholding His own Son for our good, how can we then go any longer withholding ourselves from Him?

CHAPTER 5

Broken Toenails

I HAD IT. I HAD BEEN PATIENT. I HAD BEEN LOVING. I HAD BEEN understanding, but this day, I had it. I lost it. I went crazy.

"How are you drunk right now?" I asked, amazed.

"I'm not drunk," Heidi answered.

"Yes, you are! I can see your face, and you're leaned back like you're about to fall over."

"I'm not drunk," she said with persistence.

"You were drunk when I got here this morning. I found the bottle of wine buried at the bottom of the trash can. But you sobered up. How are you drunk again?"

"Eric, I'm not drunk!"

"Oh, you're just going to lie to me like that? I'm not an idiot! You can't fool me! I've been married to you long enough to know when you lie."

"I'm not lying. I'm perfectly fine," she said with her brown eyes fixed intensely on mine, laden with a vile deadness suggesting all but our relationship was just as dead at that moment.

"Fine? I hate that word. You are not fine. You don't even know what it means to be fine!"

"I'm fine," she slowly counters with a strangled growl.

"Why? Why does this keep happening? You know better than this! We have talked about this for years in counseling and you still won't stop! We meet with a therapist once a week to figure out this one moment! This one moment when you lose awareness and drink without thinking of the consequences! Why?"

"I don't know."

"I'm sick of it! You're not trying anymore!"

"I am trying!" she shouted back.

"I trusted you yesterday and today, and this how you show me you're a trustworthy person? Forget that!"

"I am trustworthy!" she shouted again.

"You can't trick me into trusting you. Just because you say you're not drunk doesn't make it true."

Without thinking I roared, "You've ruined my life!"

She grits her teeth with a clenched jaw. With her heavy brown eyes fixed and squinted, she gave me a piercing look and replied with a like sharpness, "You're ruining your own life!"

Later, brooding over our abhorrent and crass conversation, I concluded Heidi had been right. I had allowed a vortex of my own to form in my own life. From my own hurt, I swirled. This was a vortex fueled by my sheer bitterness and resentment. I thought I had been forgiving Heidi, thinking my bitterness was only toward God. But the truth was I was merely telling myself I was forgiving just to regain a sense of normalcy with her. Simply put, she had been right. My refusal to forgive her was hurting me way more than anything she was doing. I was ruining my own life because I was allowing a root of bitterness to take hold and grow within me.

Since I continued to refuse forgiveness, any time there would be a mess up on Heidi's part, it brought back roaring to the surface all the personal hurt from previous lies. With that reopening of an ever-increasing wound, there arose an ever-mounting rush of anger. The longer I went on without forgiving Heidi, the more intense the rush became. The bitterness had built up and I lost it that day. In an uncontrollable rush of anger and hurt, I exploded.

Forgiving is hard for many reasons. One big reason I believe forgiving to be so hard is that forgiving feels unjust, and we crave justice. We love stories of revenge and justice. We love seeing the bad guy get repaid in the end for his evil. We love payback. We love classics like the *Count of Monte Cristo* and famous lines of revenge, such as "My name is Inigo Montoya. You killed my father. Prepare to die" from *The Princess Bride*. We can't forget Julia Roberts's "Big mistake" line in *Pretty Woman*. I realize these movies just might have dated me.

It doesn't matter if it is years of plotting finally coming to fruition, exacting your revenge on the six-fingered man, or showing off what people missed out on by writing you off, we love revenge. We love the satisfaction of seeing the wrong made right because deep down we want all the wrongs we've experienced to be made right. The satisfaction, however, doesn't last because whatever the "right" is that has been made, it will never erase the hurt of the wrong experienced. Killing the six-fingered man did not bring Inigo Montoya's father back, and exacting your revenge won't replace or erase the hurt you are suffering. The only thing you can do is the most unjust thing you can imagine: forgive. To release the debt. To let it go.

This leads to another reason forgiving others is so hard to practice: entitlement. Who wants to let it go? We are entitled to this. We are entitled to our grudge, anger, and bitterness. We've been wronged, we've been hurt, and we are entitled to hold onto our bitterness because we are the victims. We feel justified in our anger because we are the casualty of someone else's hurtful words or actions. To let our grudge go and forgive would be to let the culprit off the hook.

We feel completely justified in our own harmful behavior—our retaliatory remarks—which we desperately hope will land with laser pinpoint precision to ease some of our pain. Or at least even the score. We feel more than entitled to yell, "You've ruined my life!" We feel justified in hurling our resentment in the face of the one who has hurt us over and over again. Our entitlement is most obviously revealed in our blame of others. "It's your fault I don't have a job" "It's your fault money is tight." Entitlement, as an excuse to refuse forgiveness, only demonstrates our selfishness and just how far from looking like Jesus we truly are.

NO AIR SUPPORT

My first year in seminary, I was filling my car up at a gas station a few blocks from my school. It was one of those gas stations where you knew sketchy things were always going down and you only stopped there if you must. I was standing there, drenched in the Texas humidity, pumping gas when a guy in his early twenties approached me. He asked if I could give him some cash to help with his car troubles. He pointed a few pumps down to a car with its hood up and his friend shoulders deep working on the engine.

I told the guy I didn't have any cash on me, but he kept

pushing me to go to the ATM. I finally had to firmly tell him I wasn't going to help. He walked off visibly upset and I forgot about the guy. A few minutes later, after I had just sat down and shut the door to my aging air conditioner-less Honda, he shows back up at my window. I roll it down. He asks if I could at least lend him my phone to call for help since I refused to help him with money. Feeling guilty, I unlock my phone and hand it to him. He dials a friend, and about that same moment, his broken-down car abruptly stops right in front of me. I think, *Oh, good. The car is fixed.* Then the guy shoots me a great big grin and takes off to the car that had supposedly broken down. Then I calmly think, *That guy is getting in that car with my phone.* The car peels out of the station right in front of me. Then it hit me. *That guy just stole my phone!*

I peel out in pursuit. They obviously knew the area better than I did as they lost me relatively quickly. I keep pursuing frantically. I remember praying for God to take vengeance on these thuggish sinners. I was studying imprecatory psalms at the time, so naturally, I was praying for fire to come down among all other kinds of Old Testament retributions. I reminded God I was in seminary to do His will and at that moment I needed some air support.

No fire came raining down, but I did end up getting pulled over. I was glad to see the Dallas PD so I jumped out of my car to inform the officer I needed his help with my thieves. Don't ever jump out of your car when pulled over in a shady neighborhood after driving like a mad man.

A week went by before I realized these guys are not going to call me up to give me my phone back. Partly because I couldn't receive the call since they had my phone, but also why would they give it back? I also realized there would be no redeeming rain of fire—no air support from God. The debt they owed me, the debt I was entitled to be upset over, was never going to be repaid. So after that week, I let the debt go. They can keep the phone.

I was justified (in my mind) in wanting God to bring fire down on these sinners for snatching my phone. They wronged me, and I wanted vindication. I wanted my phone back. I wanted them to pay. I wanted them both to know if you mess with me, you mess with God. I was entitled to want what was rightfully mine so I was entitled to be angry when it was taken. Entitlement, however, is not a reason to refuse forgiveness.

There are many reasons we can find that makes forgiving hard, but none that exempts us from forgiving. The writer of Hebrews wrote, "See to it that no one comes short of the grace of God; that no root of bitterness springing up causes trouble, and by it many be defiled" (Hebrews 12:15 NASB). We'll talk more about this at the end of this chapter, but what we see right away is that there is a root of bitterness that can spring up in our lives. You may feel that it is unfair to forgive the one who has harmed you. You may feel entitled or justified in not forgiving the one who has hurt you, but by refusing to forgive, you water the root of bitterness inside you. The longer you go fuming and ruminating, the longer you go on fantasying and plotting your revenge, the stronger that root of bitterness grows. Quickly, after rotting you, it will spring up, poisoning those around you. The longer you fret and burn with anger, the more likely you will get hurt by doing or saying something you will regret. Take the advice of king David, who wrote,

> Trust in the LORD and do good;
> Dwell in the land and cultivate faithfulness.
> Delight yourself in the LORD;
> And He will give you the desires of your heart.
> Commit your way to the LORD,
> Trust also in Him, and He will do it.
> He will bring forth your righteousness as the light
> And your judgment as the noonday.
> Rest in the LORD and wait patiently for Him;
> Do not fret because of him who prospers in his way,
> Because of the man who carries out wicked schemes.
> Cease from anger and forsake wrath;
> Do not fret; *it leads* only to evildoing. (Psalm 37:3–7 NASB)

When we've been wronged, we are not to fret; we are to cease from anger and our pursuit of wrath. Instead, we are to occupy ourselves with doing good, growing in our character, and knowing that God is the one who will give us the desires of our heart, which in the context above is our vindication. Vindication is our wrong being made right. God will be the one who will make all things right, not us. If we become consumed with chasing down our culprit to exact our revenge, our bitterness and consuming anger will lead us to only doing evil. If we've been harmed by another, we are to wait for the Lord to make it right. In the meantime, we are to do what's right, and that means we are to forgive.

How do we do something so hard as forgive? What is the key to moving onto forgiveness, putting an end to our watering the root of bitterness that only rots us within and poisons the relationships without? How do we get past our hurt and suffering to forgive? How do we forgive in order to access what is truly ours, being altered into men and women at peace and free from bitterness?

THE KEY

It was Labor Day morning and I was about halfway to the gym when Heidi called. I answer. Through the crackling connection, I make out her saying, "Eric, you forgot your gym key." I immediately turn back because, obviously, it would make no sense to go to a gym that was locked for a holiday without the key. I had to have my key. This got me thinking of the importance of a little key. Without a key, we are locked out. Without a key, we don't have access. We may have a right to be in a certain place, a gym, office, home, but without the key, we don't have access to what is truly ours.

The word for key found in our Bible is translated from the Greek word *kleis*. This is in no way important to anything I have to say. However, another Greek word in our Bible which actually acts as a key to unlocking our ability to forgive is *kathōs*, which translates "just as." This little Greek word or English translation holds all the power for us to access our freedom from bitterness. We lead ourselves to believe that we have the right to be bitter. We deserve our rage. We are entitled to our anger. When really, we have the right to be free from our bitterness. The key that unlocks that access into our freedom and healing is kathōs—"just as."

Forgiving is not only hard but, for many, nearly impossible, especially after years of physical, psychological, or even emotional hurt. The key to unlocking that difficult door is found in the power of "just as" seen in Ephesians 4. "Let all bitterness and wrath and anger and clamor and slander be put away from you, along with all malice. Be kind to one another, tender-hearted, forgiving each other, *just as* God in Christ also has forgiven you" (Ephesians 4:31–32 NASB; emphasis added).

Paul understood bitterness and anger as emotions that belong to us, not to the one who has wronged us. This means it is our responsibility to let bitterness go, not the responsibility of the one who has harmed us. Paul says to "put away" all bitterness and anger among other things listed. How do we do this? How do we just "put away" the bitterness that has been burgeoning in us and the anger that has been blistering for years?

The first thing that will help us put away or surrender our bitterness is Paul's overall point in these two verses: we forgive because God has already forgiven us. To first get ourselves in a position to forgive, we have to remind ourselves that we once were the offenders; we once were the ones who caused harm and hurt to God. And we deserve to be punished. Fire should rain down on us. Yet God, the one unjustly crossed, has freely forgiven us in Christ Jesus and we are to do the same—*just as* He did for us. But if we have not yet grasped the depth of our sin and the length of God's grace, forgiveness will be difficult to achieve. Charles Stanley put it this way: "Once we understand the depth of our sin and the distance it put between us and God, and once we get a glimpse of the sacrifice God made to restore fellowship with us, we should not hesitate to get involved in the process of forgiveness."[15]

Be Kind

As we grow to understand the depth of our sin and the impossible debt God canceled out by His unending grace, we are emotionally ready to then take the next step in forgiving "just as" God has forgiven us. How did God forgive us? How did God cancel out the debt against us, as Paul put it in Colossians 2:14? Here, Paul says to be "kind to one another." The word for "kind" can also be translated as "gracious." How do we put away all our anger and bitterness, so that we may forgive those who have harmed or hurt us? We do so graciously because He first acted in grace toward us.

We owed God an impossible debt, yet He forgave us of the debt graciously. "For by grace you have been saved through faith; and that not of yourselves, *it is* the gift of God; not as a result of works, so that no one may boast" (Ephesians 2:8–9 NASB). I say the debt was an impossible one because there was nothing we could have done to pay the debt and keep our life at the same time. There was nothing we could have given back, worked for, or traded to pay God back the debt we owed Him and still live. "For the wages of sin is death" (Romans 6:23 NASB) and we all have sinned and fallen short, owing God death. God could have either called us on our debt or graciously forgiven it.

God chose to send His one and only Son to be the satisfactory payment for our sins. Jesus paid our debt. The death we owed God His Son paid on our behalf. However, just because Jesus has made the payment for our sins doesn't mean we have received His forgiveness. It was not until we put our faith in Jesus for eternal life that our debt was forgiven (Acts 10:43). Faith acts like a key itself, giving us access to that which is ready to be ours—forgiveness. So if we are to forgive, just as God has forgiven us, we are to live graciously toward our offenders. We either call them on the debt (which they probably can't pay back) or we graciously let the debt go, declaring they owe us nothing. *They can keep the phone.*

Tenderhearted

Describing what it looks like to be kind to one another is the word tenderhearted or compassionate. When I think of compassion, I think of putting myself in another's shoes. I think of having deep sympathy for another person. When we allow ourselves to be gracious enough to give our offender the benefit of the doubt we are more likely to extend forgiveness. The word tenderhearted in Greek means having good or strong bowels. When you have compassion for another you feel it in your gut. It breaks your heart. I am freed to forgive Heidi when I stop looking at her as a saboteur whose sole mission in life is to subvert my own. When I begin to look at her as a person who is suffering from a personality disorder, a disorder she never asked for and is trying to figure out how to navigate, compassion comes much easier. It doesn't relieve her of taking responsibility for her actions, but it does hit me in the gut, which makes forgiveness much easier for me to extend. It jabs me right in the stomach and breaks my heart when I stop looking at what she's doing as a personal aggression and see a person scared and driven by her desperate inability at times to manage her own emotions.

A great act of compassion that led to an unthinkable plea for God's forgiveness is found at the crucifixion in Luke's gospel. Jesus is on the cross and says, "Father, forgive them; for they do not know what they are doing" (Luke 23:34 NASB). Jesus is in the middle of being crucified unjustly and He calls on God to forgive. Why? They clearly deserved not to be forgiven, but because Jesus knew they were acting in ignorance of who He was, the soldiers thinking He was a criminal, Jesus saw the situation from their vantage point and had compassion. It hit Him in the gut. It broke His heart to think that the Jews—His own people—actually thought they were doing God a service. When I would have called on God for air support to make it rain fire on my executioners, out of compassion Jesus called on God to forgive.

For us to forgive, just as God has forgiven us, we must live out the same grace and compassion shown to us toward those who have harmed us. We have to do our best to see the hurting person, not the hurtful action. Maybe your offender just lost someone very close to them and this is driving them to lash out at you. Perhaps the one who keeps harming you with their comments is suffering silently from an illness or personality disorder. Who knows? But it shouldn't take you knowing for you to forgive. It is for us to be strong in grace, always giving the benefit of the doubt, in order to forgive just as we have already been forgiven.

Back to Hebrews 12:15. The writer tells us that we are to "See to it that no one comes short of the grace of God." We are to respond to the grace we've experienced from God by extending the same grace toward others. We were God's enemies (Romans 5:10), yet He showed us the richness of His grace. How should we then live? We should see to it that we don't fall short of showing to others the grace we've been shown. "As Christians, we can no longer respond to hurts, abuse, cheating, criticism, lies, and rejection in any way other than how our Lord responds to us—with forgiveness."[16]

When we fall short of living out the same grace we enjoy toward those who have harmed us, a root of bitterness begins to grow. Its roots covertly continue to burgeon as we continue to refuse forgiveness. This root of bitterness, over time, rots us from within. We are emotionally miserable and can even become physically ill after some time. As the root of bitterness strengthens within us, it springs up, causing trouble "and by it many be defiled" (Hebrews 12:15 NASB). Our bitterness won't stay buried under the surface within us for long before it breaks forth and its fruit matures, causing trouble for us and those around us. Our bitterness unleashed will cause hurt to those close to us, defiling them and making them just as bitter as us. Bitterness will rot us on the inside and through us ruin those on the outside.

THIS IS GROSS

I was looking through old notes on my phone and came across one I jotted down over a year ago. "Broken toenails: toenails break when we fight." To give a little context to this bizarre note, you need to remember I can't bend my right leg. So naturally, I can't reach my toenails on my right foot to trim them. Gross. I know. Heidi, however, graciously assumes this task. (All my previous girlfriends are thanking Jesus they dodged this bullet not marrying me.) But when Heidi and I fight, I won't ask for her to trim them. It's not that I think she will cut a toe off, but having someone else trim your toenails takes a great bit of humility and involves a great deal of intimacy. When we hold onto our anger toward another person, we are holding them at a distance. It is really hard to hold a person at a distance, wanting to cling to my bitterness, and then also have them do something as intimate as trim my toenails. This is why my toenails break when we fight. I know I can't hold onto my bitterness and still ask her to trim my toenails. I either hold on to my bitterness or I surrender it, putting it away and forgiving her. Then asking her to forgive me. (Then asking her to trim my toenails.)

I remember the night I jotted that note down in my phone. Heidi and I were in an intense screaming match for what felt like that whole evening. There was no resolution, just a cease-fire because of exhaustion. She fell asleep, but I was still fuming. I couldn't sleep. I don't remember what we were fighting about, and I don't remember what I was doing up, but as I walked out of the bedroom and stepped onto the tile floor, my toenail broke. My pride broke along with it. I sat down and typed into my phone, "Broken toenails: toenails break when we fight." What I should have typed into my phone was "Broken toenails: toenails break when we *don't forgive*."

Toenails don't just break after one or two fights. For a toenail to break—and believe me I know—it has to go untrimmed for a very long time. This means I held onto my anger and resentment for a long period of time. As my bitterness grows, my toenails grow. During this time, the root of bitterness grew also within me.

Without surrendering bitterness, it strengthens within you. It grows and festers within you. It begins to rot you. Eventually, your toenail will break because you refuse to break yourself from your bitterness by humbling yourself to graciously forgive. That is if you can't bend your leg to trim your toenails, of course.

The truth is, refusing to forgive breaks more than toenails. Choosing to not forgive breaks marriages, lifelong friendships, careers, businesses, and organizations. It breaks us of our health and happiness. It breaks you. Worst of all, refusing to forgive breaks our sense of relationship with God, and the peace and freedom therein. There is nothing we can do to break our relationship with God since it came about by grace and not works, but our *sense* of relationship, or connectedness we feel toward God, is broken when we refuse to surrender bitterness and forgive.

Who do you need to forgive? A spouse? A friend? Yourself? Could it be the case that you place some blame on God? Is your sense of relationship with God broken? Does He feel as if He is some sort of cosmic culprit who has sabotaged your happiness? He's supposed to love you and protect you, but does the overwhelming pain you feel leave you with an even greater pain—the sense that God has betrayed you in some way?

Suffering of any kind always robs us of something. There is always a loss of some kind when suffering arises. The loss of a family member, health, career, sense of peace, or comfort. Something is always taken from us when suffering blindsides us. Whatever the loss, it leaves us feeling owed, entitled, thirsty for vindication. The longer we allow these feelings to persist, the more bitter we become and the more its root grows within us.

God is ultimately the one who has the final say on all suffering. God is the one who allowed the suffering in the first place. God is the one who took your little girl home. God is the one who put a stop to you finishing school so you could take care of an ill parent. God is the one who could have healed the mental illness but didn't. God has the ultimate say in all matters, so He ultimately is the one we feel, deep down, owes us. Many times, as a result, we direct our bitterness toward Him. For many, this is exactly why they are done with God. A God that would allow such personal hurt is a God they refuse to forgive. Their sense of relationship never mends as they hold onto their bitterness.

Perhaps your bitterness toward God has grown out of a tiny root into a full-blown, bitter-fruit-producing tree that has rotted you within and caused so much harm and bitterness to take root in those around you. The key to forgiving God, or releasing Him from whatever debt you believe He owes you, is coming to terms with the truth that God owes you nothing. Everything He does is for our good, even if it doesn't feel or look like it. It is hard to imagine but whatever hurt He is allowing, somehow, is ultimately for our good.

The fact of the matter is that we are the ones who should feel indebted to God for the forgiveness we have found freely in Christ. We must remind ourselves that whatever our loss, it is somehow for our good because we have a good God. As hard as it may be, thank God. Ask Him to strengthen you in your suffering. Surrender your bitterness and let God off your hook. "You must not keep it in and you must not share it. Surrender it to the Father, through the Son."[17]

Before we can surrender our bitterness and forgive others the debt we feel is owed us, we have to know first what it means to surrender ourselves. We will never be spiritually in a place where we will be able to surrender our bitterness and release others—even God—from the insurmountable pain we suffer until we learn how to first surrender ourselves to Jesus.

If we want to be radically altered into looking and loving like Jesus, we must be just as Hs is—a person who radically forgives. To radically forgive, we must do something as radical as surrender ourselves over to a good and just God, just as Jesus did in His suffering. When we learn to surrender ourselves, with all our wants and desires, we learn to surrender our entitlement and desire for revenge we so vindictively want to hold onto. When we forgive others we are not letting them off the hook for what they've said or done; we are only letting them off *our* hook. To surrender our bitterness and forgive, we have to surrender ourselves first.

To be people who have been radically altered by God's grace, we must first not fall short of living out that radical grace toward others. The grace we've been shown, we must also show. The compassion we've been given, we must also give. The forgiveness we enjoy we must also employ. Remember God, and all He has forgiven you, then you will be able to supernaturally forgive some of the most impossible debts. In doing so, all will see through the suffering that has drastically altered your life, God is radically altering you.

CHAPTER 6

Lose Yourself before You Lose Yourself

T HE LIGHTS IN THE CHURCH AUDITORIUM FLICKERED ON TO their full brightness from their previously dimmed setting. I get up from my front row seat and climbed the four or five steps up to the top of the stage on that early October morning. The room smelled of coffee and upholstered chairs; the atmosphere hung in a subtle anticipation as always before a sermon. As I open my Bible and settle in behind the pulpit I hear faint whispers and the sporadic cough. The sermon I was moments away from preaching centered on the question "How do we follow Jesus when He's leading us where we do not want to go?" This sermon was more personal for me than usual. I had been wrestling with this exact question for months. I knew God was in control, but everything was very much out of my control. This is usually your sign God is asking you to follow Him to a place you don't want to go, a place of complete dependence on Him. I had been in a dog fight to avoid following Him. A fight I was about to lose.

By October, the self-destructive nature of Heidi's BPD had progressed. I didn't even recognize her anymore. She looked the same, kind of, but she wasn't the person I married. Her behavior, even when not drinking, was unpredictable. She wasn't the annoyingly happy girl I dated whose affectionate nickname was Motormouth. Now her motormouth needed a hard-core governor. By this point, our problem was obvious to those around us, which only made the prefrontal cortex vortex worse. Heidi was saying absurd things about me and others in a desperate attempt to deflect the increasing attention off herself.

As a result of my intense control over Heidi's ability to access alcohol, the only outlet she could find to quiet the whispering voices of shame in her head had become the easily accessible hand sanitizer. Like mentioned before, it was during this time that most likely resulted in the disconnection of her prefrontal cortex.

So Heidi, in part, stopped accessing the section of her brain that thinks, *Stop talking. That's not polite.* And *Don't do that. You will hurt yourself.* As a result, her life was turning into a vortex, swirling faster and faster, sucking in me and anyone who ventured too close. She and I were both in a death spiral together, and I was terrified of what was crouched there at the bottom waiting.

I preached the sermon knowing this end was coming; knowing that however hard it had been up to this point what awaited us was going to be even more difficult. I think I was preaching to myself. I was hoping to encourage myself or find some life somehow. I knew Jesus was leading me to a place where I did not want to go. The unknown and inevitability of that place haunted me. Our shadow grew wider as we plummeted.

The crash was coming. I didn't know, however, it was only a month away.

So how do you follow Jesus when He is asking you to go with Him somewhere you do not want to go? A place where only pain and suffering will greet you? A place where grief and loss are anxious to become old friends? A month before the sermon, I was up early praying and reading. My resentment and bitterness had come to a foamy, fuming head. God was not ruling my life how I believed He ought to be ruling. I was irritated by all Heidi was doing, but I was incensed with God for all that He wasn't doing.

As my resentment grew stronger upward to God, my envy stretched further outward of others. Every time I got on Twitter or Instagram, I saw another pastor with his wife showcasing their awesome God-blessed ministry, their success, and their happiness together. They loved their jobs and were thriving (or so it appeared). My intense bitterness toward God hurled me deeper into the cycle of bitterness and envy. Bitterness toward God and envy of others. Every go-around increasingly getting stronger and stronger.

I got up early on September 2, went into Heidi's office, shut the double doors behind me, and let God have it. I've always been a believer that God is bigger than my frustrations, so I let Him have it at times. This was one of those times. I'm naming off all these other pastors and listing their accomplishments and advancements since seminary. I'm asking God why He called me into ministry if He was planning on sabotaging it all along. He's God. He knew this was going to happen. Why did He string me along? Why did He give me a passion for seeing lives radically altered by His grace, only to drastically alter my life into disappointment and crushed dreams? I felt like the prophet

Jeremiah. God had coaxed me into ministry and I had let him with my own apparitions of achievement and advancement.

I'm in a fury as I pray. *Why can't she love You more than stupid hand sanitizer? Why am I even a youth pastor? I never took a class on youth ministry! Why did You bring me to this town and murder my ministry? This is Your idea of eternal life? Why did I ever say that I would do whatever and go wherever for You? That was a mistake!* As my bitterness boiled that morning, it was as if God were my therapist, quietly sitting and listening on the love seat next to the desk I sat, letting me unload.

Somewhere in the raging and in my intense envy, I said, "Why do all these pastors have it so good and I'm forgotten by You?" Right then, it was as if God, who had been comfortably lounging on the sofa, suddenly sat forward and interrupted my pity party. I thought, *Didn't you calculate the cost?* I stopped, and Luke 14 immediately popped into my mind. I opened my Bible and read a discipleship passage from Jesus. "For which one of you, when he wants to build a tower, does not first sit down and calculate the cost to see if he has enough to complete it?" (Luke 14:28 NASB).

I wanted to follow Jesus, but I didn't account for where all He might lead me. I had been credulous to believe that He would only lead me beside still waters (which He literally did, we live in a town called Stillwater) and blind to the shadow of death part. Perhaps I just convinced myself that the "shadow of death" part wasn't for me. Jesus goes on to say at the end of His teaching, "So then, none of you can be My disciple who does not give up all his own possessions" (Luke 14:33 NASB). I wanted to be His disciple, but I wanted all the things I treasured as well. I wanted a big, pretty ministry. I wanted to be able to flash around on social media my pretty marriage and family like other pastors. I wanted to be someone in ministry. But my borderline blonde blew it all up. And God allowed it.

At the beginning of this passage, Jesus says, "If anyone comes to Me, and does not hate his own father and mother and wife and children and brothers and sisters, yes, and even his own life, he cannot be My disciple" (Luke 14:26 NASB). Yes, even his own life. I loved my own life and I hated God for ruining it. So I shot back at God, *What about the other pastors who have it easy compared to me? They look like they don't hate their life.* Right then, I thought, *What's it to you? You follow me.* I flipped in my Bible from Luke to the end of John's gospel. Jesus has just told Peter that when he grows old, he will stretch out his hands and someone else will tie them and lead him to a place he does not want to go. Peter turns around and sees another disciple, John, and asks, "What about him?" Jesus, replies to Peter, "What *is that* to you? You follow Me!" (John 21:22 NASB).

I got it. I didn't like it, but I got it. God was not merely allowing a mental illness to take my wife. He was not allowing it to take my ministry. God does not merely allow our suffering; God calls us into suffering. He is calling us to follow Him at the cost of our own life. You cannot be a disciple and not suffer. The very act of surrendering your life, losing your life to gain it, is what it means to suffer. The loss of anything is to suffer, but especially the loss of our own life. He's calling us to follow Him at the loss of our ministries and careers, at the loss of all the treasures we hold near and dear.

Our specific suffering didn't just accidentally happen to Heidi and me, to drastically alter our lives from everything we had planned; we believe God appointed it. Though God appoints suffering at times in the Bible this is not always the case. What is always the case when suffering arises is that God appoints us. He calls us to something bigger than the pursuit of our own happiness and comfort. Through the call to suffer, God is calling us to hate our own life by loving His more—more than our father and mother and wife and children and brothers and sisters. We are to reject even our own lives because they are not anything in comparison to His life in us.

WHEN CHRIST COMES CALLING

As I sat through my two-hour crash course on codependency, I seriously wondered how I wasn't codependent. I had never heard of codependency until that day. There were all kinds of codependency descriptions, definitions, and patterns listed in black on the dry-erase board in this particular room. Some things listed were "an absence of personal boundaries." I thought, *Yes.* "An 'outer-focused' locus of control." *Yes.* "Pleasing, 'protecting' others, zero boundaries or relating 'behind walls.'" *Yep.* I fit these and just about everything else written on the board. I noticed as the codependency discussion went on that I met just about all the characteristics, except the main one. I hadn't lost my sense of selfhood.

Regarded as an authority on the subject, Melody Beattie defines a codependent in her book, *Codependency No More,* as a person "who has let another person's behavior affect him or her, and who is obsessed with controlling that person's behavior."[18] Beattie draws attention to the codependent's obsessive need to control and rescue (among other things) the destructive person. Codependents often find themselves then drawn to others who are addicted or dysfunctional because they've lost their selfhood to the extent that they need to be needed. In a sense, the codependents become addicts themselves, becoming addicted to the addict at the neglect of their own well-being. They lose themselves in an attempt to save another.

Some, on the other hand, don't believe codependency is a disorder at all. In his book *Clean*, David Sheff refers to research that seems to indicate "that codependence is neither a discrete disorder nor a manifestation of an underlying psychiatric disorder."[19] It is simply how any rational person would respond to the irrationality of their loved one's destructive behavior. Logic does not work when trying to love and help a person whose illogical destructive behavior is so baffling. As already mentioned, a major trait of BPD is self-destructive behavior. Self-destructive behavior is, in and of itself, illogical and baffling. Sheff's point is that anyone who gets caught in the vortex of a loved one's self-destructive behavior would naturally look as if they themselves had a disorder. Living with an addict or a person with a personality disorder will make you, at the very least, look like you have a disorder of your own.

What if we all, in a sense, are "codependent" to our careers, health, beauty, or spouse? What if we are losing ourselves to or into these? What if we are becoming obsessed with any number of things to the point we've lost ourselves? The danger of deriving a false sense of self-hood and well-being from things or people, is that when we lose them we will lose ourselves; we will lose our sense of self-hood and well-being along with them.

So, just like a person who has become dependent on another, has lost himself or herself, all of us likewise are in danger. We will lose ourselves if we have made our life dependent upon our job, our spouse, our 401(k), etc. These are not capable of being enduring sources of life for us. Yet, it is not out of the question for us to make any one of these a false source of our self-worth, peace, and security. A job, however great it may be, was never meant to be your source of significance. A spouse, however great he or she may be, was never meant to be your sole source of love. Or the sole object of your love. Your 401(k), regardless of how big, was never meant to be your source of financial peace and future security. Your physical health, regardless of how strong you are, was never meant to be the source of your confidence. The immovable God is your source for all these. All others are removable and suffering the loss of any one of these false sources of happiness in life can result in a loss of your life—your sense of self.

Jesus teaches us that unless we lose ourselves by making God the one and only source of our peace, security, self-worth, we are already lost; we just don't realize it. And many of us won't realize it until suffering exposes our need for God to be our true source for life. It is not beyond God to use suffering the loss of any one of our false sources of life to reveal to us our improper dependence upon them and our true need for Him. C. S. Lewis asked it this way: "While what we call 'our own life' remains agreeable we will not surrender it to Him. What then can God do in our interest but make 'our own life' less agreeable to us, and take away the plausible source of false happiness?"[20]

Jesus came to give life and to give it abundantly. That abundant life is not you desperately scrambling around, hustling day after day to try and save your life as you know it. The abundant life is the present, tangible, joy we find when we surrender our life as we know it. Hear me clearly: the abundant life Jesus gives is not a relax on the beach kind of life. It isn't the "American dream" kind of life either. The abundant life isn't blissful circumstances or blessings beyond belief; it has its fair share of hurts and troubles. The abundant life is discovering a joy in Jesus that is not seen in anything else.

Jesus gives life freely to all who would believe in Him for it, but the abundance of that life received by faith—the quality of that life—is experienced only as we, by faith, surrender over more and more of our selfish wants and desires to Him. It is experienced as we surrender over our false sources of life to make more room for the preeminence of His life. If we are chasing a life as we believe it is *supposed to* be, we will be pressured to control circumstances and fix others around us who are sabotaging that belief from becoming a reality. We must stop chasing life as we believe it is *supposed to* be and start trusting in *the Life* for how He wants us to be.

As believers, we all are supposed to respond to the call of discipleship. Our life was buried with Christ, and as He was raised from the dead, we too have been raised to walk in a new life. However, so many believers still cling to the old life, succumbing to the illusion that somehow their new life in Christ is still their own. You may not like this, but your life is not your own. Many believers are missing the point today and the point is to answer the call to discipleship. A call to die. As a result of missing the call—or now possibly rejecting the call—many are missing out on discovering the unforeseen joy of the abundant life. It is sad that so many of us possess eternal life, but instead of choosing to experience the abundance of that life, we'd rather choose to experience anything and everything else this world seems to serve up with a pretty garnish.

Suffering is a way God makes the call clear again for many of us who are missing it. Answering that call awakens us to experience the quality of the eternal life we gained the moment we trusted in Christ. Only when we answer the call, will bitterness toward God then begin to disappear and our intense envy of others dissolve. Dietrich Bonhoeffer famously penned this call and our response in his book, *The Cost of Discipleship.*

> When Christ calls a man, he bids him come and die. It may be a death like that of the first disciples who had to leave home and work to follow him, or it may be a death like Luther's, who had to leave the monastery and go out into the world. But it is the same death every time—death in Jesus Christ, the death of the old man at his call."[21]

We don't chase our dream life; we come to Jesus and die so we may experience the abundance of His dream for our life.

DO WHAT YOU HAVE TO DO

Something had to give. Something needed to happen. Something big needed to rock Heidi, to shake Heidi out of her destructive behavior. I prayed, probably every morning, "God, do what You have to do, but …" I wasn't at the place where I was just going to surrender over my wife, my children, and even my dream life to God. I would pray, "God, do what You have to do to humble Heidi, but no DUIs." Other prayers were "God, do what You have to do to wake Heidi up, but no car wrecks." "God, do what You have to do to save Heidi, but keep her reputation intact."

November rolled around. The vortex that was Heidi's life was sucking in everyone close to her. For months I could feel we were headed toward something bad. I just didn't know what it would be. I knew it would take something bad to change the course we were trapped traveling. Since September I had been wrestling with how to love Jesus more than my family. Loving Jesus meant following Him to a place I didn't want to go. I didn't know exactly what awaited me there, but I knew it would be painful. Would Heidi be diagnosed with cirrhosis? Was there to be a horrible drunken wreck? Was Heidi going to kill someone on the road? For the last two months, I wrestled with God, praying prayers like "God, do what You have to do, but ..." and "Jesus, I will follow You, just not there."

Things were not getting better. I was struggling and didn't know how I could go on much longer. On the morning of November 8, I wake up and head to Heidi's office while everyone still slept. I shut the double doors behind me and meditated on Psalm 91.

> Because he has loved Me, therefore I will deliver him;
> I will set him *securely* on high, because he has
> known My name.
> He will call upon Me, and I will answer him;
> I will be with him in trouble;
> I will rescue him and honor him.
> With a long life I will satisfy him
> And let him see My salvation. (Psalm 91:14–16
> NASB)

I thirsted for it all. I desperately craved us to experience His deliverance. I wanted us to be set on high. Wherever "on high" is, it had to be better than the depths we had been slumming in for years. I begged for my prayers to be answered. I pleaded for God to hear me. God said to the one who loved Him that He would be with that person to rescue and honor him and satisfy him with a long life. And the icing on the cake, God would let him see His salvation. The part "I will be with him in trouble" was what I needed to hear. That morning I prayed, "God, do what You have to do." No *but* this morning. No *just not*. Only "Do what You have to do." Period.

Nothing seemed any different than the mornings before. Nothing seemed more spiritual than the prayers before. I got ready for work. I went to our staff meeting. We all went to lunch. I got things ready for that Wednesday night. Everything seemed like every day before, just another day heavy with the same tormenting task of balancing anxieties with responsibilities.

That afternoon while setting up for youth, which would be later that evening, I was texting Heidi to ease my nerves. I did this daily so I could have enough peace of mind to get things done while at work. She seemed fine. Nothing stood out to me that she was off or I should worry. Then, without warning, she goes dark. She's not responding. I finish up what I needed to have done then I leave early at 4:15.

Leaving early on Wednesday wasn't uncommon for me. I had to be right back at the church at 6:00 p.m. Most Wednesday nights I didn't get home until after 10:00 p.m. By then all the children were asleep. So leaving a little early on Wednesday was the only time I was able to see the children that day and have a little time to play with them.

I head home with my stomach in knots. With nervous palms and tense fingers, I tightly choke the steering wheel. I couldn't tell you which was wrung tighter, the wheel by my desperate grip or my stomach by the nefarious and menacing knot. The knot that coiled within me as I drove had become my all too familiar foe by this point. Always seizing me. Always ravishing me. Out of nowhere, he could appear and just take me.

As I approach my neighborhood, I see a police car pull in the entrance. Moments later I make the right hand turn into the neighborhood to see the officer getting out of his car across from my house. The familiar, horrible feeling twisting in me was now altogether something new and awful. I pull in my 45-degree angle driveway, hit the button to raise the garage door, and get out of my car as the officer is walking up the drive behind me.

"Do you live here?"

"Yes," I reply slowly.

"We received a call that the mother is intoxicated, possibly with children inside."

I think, *Great*. Then say, "Okay. Let's go check it out."

I am not going to talk about what we found as we walked into the house that day, but I'll say something supernatural took place in me. More police showed up. I thought about what God had told me that morning. *I will be with him in trouble.* As this promise kept popping in my head, I felt a strange supernatural comfort. I kept wondering *Why am I being so cool?* Where had my oppressive foe gone?

Yes, I felt anxious, but the anxiety was without dread now. The anxiety hadn't seized me, washing over me as times before. I was anxious about the moment but confident about the future. I hated what I was seeing, but I was hopeful about the change that would follow. Soon the ambulance showed up. God kept whispering to me, *I will be with him in trouble. I will be with him in trouble.* Most people would have been beside themselves. Irate. Scared. Even terrified. I was strangely at peace. My source of peace was in an immoveable God whose promise I had entrenched in my thinking. *I will be with him in trouble.*

When we learn to lose our life and gain Christ's, we gain the things that characterize His life. Peace, comfort, confidence in God regardless of the chaos surrounding. We gain a clearer eternal perspective. Paul said that he had been crucified with Christ and he no longer lived, but Christ lived in him. Paul goes on to write what it looks like to be crucified with Christ. He writes that we who belong to Jesus have crucified the flesh with its passions and desires. We don't live doing what we want anymore; we live doing what Jesus wants.

The flesh is the old self-centered way of thinking. It seeks only to serve itself at the expense of others and you. The flesh thinks nothing of God or what God desires for you; it thinks only of its future and its survival. The flesh works to fulfill its own passions and lusts, which are always in opposition to God's own passion and desire for us. God not only promises to be with us, but He jealously desires for us to be with Him (James 4:5).

WHAT'S IT TO YOU?

So back to the question "How do you follow Jesus when He's leading you where you do not want to go?" After all this is what disciples do, they follow Jesus. This is what Jesus is calling us all to do, no matter the cost. So when He appears reckless and careless, allowing you to undergo all the hurt and confusion, how do you follow Him? When what you are embarking upon is so scary, how do you confidently set out to follow Jesus into the unknown? I will develop this more but our only step at this point is to surrender.

In our culture, the word *surrender* is a bad word. We don't surrender. We don't give up. Even our family motto is "Austins Never Give Up." Throughout history, we have great stories of men and women who, when faced with the choice of surrender or die, chose to fight until the bitter end. Heroes choose death; cowards surrender to save their own life. It's cowardly to give up and come walking out with your hands up. "Hands up" is the universal sign for loser. Winners sacrifice it all—even themselves—for the win. Heroes sacrifice it all for the cause, so why is surrender the big secret to following Jesus?

When we talk about surrendering being the secret to following Jesus, we're talking about it in the same paradoxical sense that Jesus did. Surrender doesn't mean saving your own life (as we typically think of it) but losing it. We don't surrender to save our life, we surrender sacrificing our life itself. To make this sacrifice means to hoist it high upon the proverbial cross. It is valuing His life as preeminent to our own. If we are going to take that first step in following Jesus into the dark, scary unknown of cancer or the unknown of a spouse's potential affair, we have to choose death, not life. By faith we sacrifice; we choose to surrender that old life with its dreams and desires. We surrender how we pictured our family, health, or our careers, believing that whatever is on the other side of our suffering (or even in our suffering) is better because God is leading us there. It takes great courage of faith to surrender all you've worked for, all you care for, just to know Jesus more and to offer yourself upon the altar of the unknown to be radically altered by Him. Whatever loss your suffering has brought you, you will never be able to entrust it in order to endure it, unless you have already learned how to surrender or entrust yourself.

Suffering has a profound way of showing us that we are losing; we may be losing control, losing dreams, or losing our sense of peace. Pain makes it clear we can no longer do this life on our own. We surrender and let go of this life so we don't have to do it alone. We walk out with our hands up, not to save our own life, but to gain the joy of His (John 15:11). When we lose, we become true winners. When we lose our life, we win the supernatural joy that comes from His life flowing through us and out of us. We discover a joy that no hurt or pain can touch. We discover a joy unforeseen.

When we surrender ourselves, when we lose our old selves, we gain the experience of our new selves in Jesus. Our new selves cannot be lost because we've already been found in Christ. We are not in danger of losing ourselves any longer if we lose our job. We are not in danger of losing ourselves if we lose our spouse. We no doubt suffer loss, but we will not suffer the loss of our new selves or the abundant life found in our new self—the experience of our new life. No amount of suffering can bring us a loss of identity because we've already surrendered the things we have, for so long, used to derive our false sense of peace and significance, our false sense of self-worth and self-hood. We become content with saying, "Do what You have to do. Period." No *but*. No *just not*. No hesitations or compromises. Just surrender of ourselves to Him and His plan, no matter how scary.

When you realize you can't lose something you've already lost, you may still feel fear and anxiety but you begin to experience peace and comfort in the midst of the fear and anxiety. You can't dread losing something you've already surrendered over to an immovable God. You can't lose your dream life if you've already traded it in for His dream for your life. You've surrendered the dream. You've surrendered the wife, the husband, the teen, the career, or the diagnosis to Jesus. You are surrendering you when you start entrusting yourself and it all to Him. When Jesus teaches discipleship, He teaches us to pick up our cross and follow Him. To pick up our cross means to die to ourselves—to lose ourselves. A. W. Tozer put it this way in his book *The Root of the Righteous*:

> So the cross not only brings Christ's life to an end, it ends also the first life, the old life, of every one of His true followers. It destroys the old pattern, the Adam pattern, in the believer's life, and brings it to an end. Then the God who raised Christ from the dead raises the believer and a new life begins.[22]

A big step toward losing ourselves to Jesus is sacrificing the delusion of control we have come to believe we exercise over our own lives. Some areas of our life we fight to maintain rulership may run contrary to what God desires for us, such as our marriage, our family, our standard of living, our retirement, and our careers. Surrender doesn't mean we abandon them all; we simply go to Jesus in prayer and tell Him it's all His now. Do what You have to do.

God, You want me to have a career change? Okay, lead the way because I don't know the next step. You are the ruler over my career, not me.

God, You want me to stay with my unfaithful spouse? If I do, I'll need all Your strength to do what I don't want to do, to go into this painful process I don't want to go. You are the ruler over my marriage, not me.

When we throw our hands up and make the ultimate sacrifice of surrendering ourselves, we gain the overwhelming experience of His life pumping through us. When we end our life set on selfish wants, desires, and passions and let His life take over, then we see miracles worked through us. We see our marriages altered. We see our careers altered. We see people jump out of practicing law and medicine to jump into ministry. We see people jump out of ministry and jump into practicing something else entirely. Whatever God wants, He gets, in order to bring justice and healing to others and us. He ultimately gets what He wants, and what He wants is His people looking like His Son. If not in this life, then for sure at the resurrection.

God, however, doesn't want you to wait until then to experience His life, which is in you now. He wants you to experience that newness of life, that resurrected life, now by losing yourself before you lose yourself to the empty sources in this world we so often look to for our sense of peace and security. Being a disciple then must now be viewed not merely in terms of following Jesus, but a willingness to leave everything behind for Jesus. If we are willing to leave behind everything, then we will be willing to lose anything if Jesus asks. Whether it be nets, the family business, or a dream. When we follow Jesus we are leaving behind what we want for what He wants, ready to surrender anything when He asks because we've already surrendered everything, including ourselves.

Almost a week after what we nefariously refer to as "November

8," Heidi and I were driving into the desert to check her into rehab. For days, Psalm 91:15 kept popping into my head. *I will be with him in trouble.* We arrived at the lush, rustic facility. After we finalized the payment, I carried Heidi's bags as we followed the admission counselor down the path through a tranquil scene of palm trees, towering cacti, and Tuscan buildings. Our stride was as relaxed as the atmosphere. We were accompanied on our walk through the oasis by the calming sounds of rippling water and the soft rustle of palms above. The warm sun perfectly melded with the gentle breeze as the two met our faces. We would arrive too soon at the nurses' station where Heidi would undergo her physical and psychological evaluation.

My paradisiacal feelings, however, did not meld so nicely with my feelings of apprehension. As tranquil of a scene as it was, it did not fully disarm me of the unease I felt leaving Heidi among strangers. I scanned the ornate landscape of palms trees and soaring cacti, hyper-vigilantly looking for patients giving me the "Don't do it. Run!" look. I didn't see any runners or SOS signals. If we were going to bail because of something sketchy, now was the time. I saw nothing alarming but still on edge as we walked into the nurse's station, nestled on the far side of the entrancing campus. It was a small but comfortable waiting room with a few empty chairs lining the wall in front of us and an empty nurse's desk to the right. Opposite of the desk was a door. Out form this door two nurses warmly walked out to greet us. Now was the time to say our goodbyes. The workers step aside to give us some privacy. As we hug, I tell her she is courageous for getting help. It takes courage to surrender. I fought back the tears then like I'm doing now as I write this. I kiss her, then say goodbye. She turns to follow the nurses through the door. As soon as she does, the door lazily closes between us.

I drove north to Phoenix for the night. The dying sun burned bright as it shot forth its golden rays over the silhouetted mountain peaks. The sun's sinking presence littered rocky shadows along the desert terrain. The now fading sun refused surrender. In hopes to delay the downward pull of its final moments, its beams reached helplessly upward toward the sky. Without surprise, the glowing sun slowly yielded to the mountains' draw; and as it quietly drowned into the mountain seal it cast upward upon the now altered sky, and its relaxed clouds, the most lustrous yellow hue and delicate shades of pink and blue. The fleeting moments of such a beautiful spectacle brought a sense of calm and comfort.

Before bed, I sat under the soft cover of a single lamp praying for Heidi while scared for her in a new place with strangers for the first time. I didn't know if the people who worked at the facility would treat her well. I didn't know if the other patients would be kind and welcome her. I didn't know if she would sit alone in the cafeteria. I didn't know if her roommate would kill her. I hated that she was alone. I hated I couldn't be with her. Then it popped in my head again, perhaps the most overlooked promise in the Bible, *I will be with him in trouble.*

Matthew uses this promise to bookend his gospel. The angel shows up to tell Mary she will have a son and His name shall be called Immanuel, which translated means "God with us." Then at the end of Matthew's gospel, Jesus gives the promise "I am with you always, even to the end of the age" (Matthew 28:20 NASB). Immanuel, God with us, promises to always be with us, even until the end of the age, which includes our times of trouble. I went on from Matthew and read another well-known verse. "I will never desert you, nor will I ever forsake you" (Hebrews 13:5 NASB).

God was with Heidi, and as the next verse goes on to say because God will never leave us or forsake us, we can confidently say, as we commit to endure, "The Lord is my helper I will not be afraid." The more mature our faith grows, the more strength and confidence we gain because we come to know Him more; we come to experience Him truly as our helper. We can have the confidence to follow Jesus to places we don't want to go because we know He, Immanuel, will stick it out with us while there. We know once we arrive at the scary place Jesus is leading us, we have the ultimate helper. We may have anxiety, but it will be without dread because the Lord is our helper. We may be scared, but it will be without terror because the Lord is our helper.

The next day, I boarded an airplane for Oklahoma. I sat in my seat, looking out the plane window. As soon as the wheels left the pavement, I began crying quietly so as not to be heard. I prayed. I begged. I pleaded with God to cure Heidi. I did so very quietly because it is weird when people cry next to you on a plane. As Phoenix became smaller and smaller below me out my plane window, I hurt more and more for Heidi.

Heidi and I rarely were apart. The longest may have been a few days while she was on a business trip, but nothing like thirty days. She was alone, but she wasn't. Immanuel, God, was with her. So although I hurt for her, I was no longer afraid for her. I believed this was God doing what He had to do like I had prayed. No longer wishing to refuse surrender, the promise I read "I will be with him in trouble" had become a beautiful spectacle that brought me a sense of calm and comfort. Now was the time I believed God would begin to radically alter our lives. We were helpless and the next steps seemed murky, but we were confident because God was in the murk with us and He, the Lord, is our helper.

When we lose ourselves to God, we open ourselves up to God's transformative work within us. Losing ourselves is really us just getting out of the way of Him having His way with us. As this transformative work increases, we gain a radically altered spiritual perspective and experience. We can go through the most terrifying, hand-wringing, gut-wrenching of times and our anxiety be without dread. We can acknowledge the anxious thoughts but enjoy the strange peace.

The enjoyment of this strange peace is possible because it is rooted in our confidence of a loving, immoveable God. And since He's immovable, the peace found in Him is immovable. We can feel alone yet know we are never alone. We are surprised, being met by the strange joy and peace only God can give while we suffer. Although we hate the pain, we begin to gratefully experience God in a way we didn't even know was possible. This is when you begin to see your life, which was drastically altered by suffering, start to become radically altered by God's grace.

So what's it to you? Do you want to surrender and follow Jesus, even when He is leading you to places you don't want to go? Do you want to leave behind the things that falsely promise life to follow Jesus and experience His joy made full in you? Or, do you want to keep looking behind at others, wishing you had what they had? Do you want to keep clinging to the control you never really had? As your suffering overtakes you, are you going to continue to helplessly reach for the delusion of omnipotence you think you wield? Do you want to keep on being discontent with what you do have and envious of what you don't?

What do you want to be the source of your peace and the guardian of your security? Do you want an immovable God or something that is here today but could be gone tomorrow? Do you want the inconsistent and empty promises of this life or an everlasting Rock? Will you continue defaulting to doubting God's goodness when it falsely appears He's robbed you of your happiness? It's your choice: Look back and long for the life that is already lost or look forward to Jesus and endure for the life that is already yours? Are you ready to lose yourself to Jesus before you lose yourself to the false sources of life in this world? Jesus asks, "For what is a man profited if he gains the whole world, and loses or forfeits himself?" (Luke 9:25 NASB). We must learn to lose ourselves before we lose ourselves. This means we follow Jesus no matter the cost. No matter how thick the darkness or heavy the hurt that lay ahead of you, Jesus is telling you, "Follow Me."

CHAPTER 7

Desert Mirage

M Y LANDING IN ARIZONA MID-DECEMBER WAS MUCH BETTER
than my departure had been a month earlier. For the past
three weeks, while Heidi had been in rehab, she seemed to have
found herself again. For the past three weeks we talked every
day, twice most days. She looked great over FaceTime. I wasn't
just excited to see her; I was excited to see the person I knew
before all this mess. She also found a community that would
be incredibly hard to leave. She had met people with whom she
would never have crossed paths before and now would have
to leave.

I landed, picked up my Mitsubishi Mirage from the car rental,
and headed to my hotel. I had gone out to Arizona the week
before Heidi finished her thirty-day program to participate in
Family Week. Family Week at this particular treatment facility
was Monday through Friday.

The day began with an orientation and tour, then straight
into coursework. Among other courses, this is where I had my
crash course on codependency I mentioned earlier. The week was

not only a time for family members to gain an understanding of how their loved one was suffering but also a time for healing, forgiving, and reconciling if possible by the week's end. It's a time when families can deal with hurtful issues that substance abuse and/or mental illness created in the past. A time to mend rifts and restore relationships once bulldozed. One of the ideas behind the week is that once there is a better understanding of how a person's loved one is suffering through coursework, compassion would then open the door to forgiveness. A large part of the time dealt with what is called *list work*. List work aided us in safely bringing to the surface painful issues and then constructively walking us through the process of mending the tattered relationship.

Once the work had been completed and the week was over, we could move forward with a fresh start toward recovery, if possible. Some relationships, however, were already destroyed. Family members or spouses didn't even bother to show up. Some relationships were hanging by a thread, and still others were hopeful. We were hopeful. I was hopeful for healing. I was ready for healing. Now, more than ever, it seemed like healing was for once very possible. That week I was getting the first taste of what it would be like to have Heidi back for good. But healing doesn't come easily. Sometimes God doesn't work as fast as we would like. Sometimes He doesn't work at all how we would like.

BROKEN-DOWN MIRAGE

Friday had finally come. We finished up our work that morning, then headed to lunch. Heidi said her goodbyes while I loaded up the Mirage. We hit the interstate and headed south, eventually curving back to the east to go through New Mexico. I still couldn't get over how great Heidi looked. For the first time, after a very long time, it felt as if I finally had her back. We both were excited to see each other. Heidi filled me in on all kinds of stories and fun she had with friends she made over the past month. Again, I couldn't get over how great she looked. Physically she was in great shape. The hand sanitizer had done quite the damage to her white blood cells, especially her neutrophils (a subset of white cells). When a person's neutrophils get too low, that person can suffer serious infections from basic bacterial infections.

Mentally, she was all there; she was back to Heidi. She was happy and carefree. I remember being happy as well. As we drove through the desert, I soaked in how beautiful she looked. She sat leaned back in her seat with her feet up on the dash; her toes pointed forward. Out the window, her arm races past the desert cliffs. Her opened hand slightly lifts and falls against the warm air's drag. Reflecting in her recently purchased sunglasses, the boulders brilliantly burned with a beautiful rust colored glow. *Had rehab worked?* I thought. Everything I had learned during Family Week and the recent years of betrayal had me skeptical. I wanted to believe what I saw. I wanted to hope but was hesitant to get my hopes up because I knew first-hand the concussing blow of disappointment. All that mattered for that moment, though, was that the stranger sitting next to me was gone, and my wife was back in the passenger seat.

The desert sun had advanced and it was now twilight. The brilliant glow of the desert boulders were starting to no longer beam off Heidi's lenses when all of a sudden, *boom!* Flat tire. I pull over to inspect, and sure enough, the back right tire was flat. No worries, I know how to fix a flat. I had hoped to get to Albuquerque at a decent time so we could go out somewhere special to celebrate Heidi completing her program, so I had to work fast.

The Mitsubishi Mirage is small and its back was loaded down with our suitcases, things Heidi had made, and clothes that I had shipped to her from Oklahoma. (She had not accounted for the drastic change in temperature of the desert when she first packed.) We had to unload the small Mirage to get to the spare tire. Finally, we got it all out. I fixed the flat, loaded the small Mirage back up, and we were back on the road. As we took off, I joked about us being a broken-down mirage in the desert. After we laughed at my lame joke, all of a sudden, *boom.* It hit me. *What if this is all a mirage? What if her recovery is just an illusion and when we get back to Oklahoma this mirage breaks down and she goes back to her old behavior?*

Decembers in Oklahoma are far from Decembers in Arizona. I couldn't help but worry about taking her from sunny, warm Arizona, where she had made so much progress, to cold, dank Oklahoma where magnificent colors are dulled by the gloomy clouds of winter. I felt like I was setting her up for relapse. I, of course, didn't share these thoughts with Heidi. I had recently learned that even if we had our doubts about our loved one's recovery, we were to never show them our doubts, but always give them our confidence.

We made it to Albuquerque, but not at a decent time. We hit up the Fridays next door to take back to our hotel room. Not the celebratory dinner I had imagined. We ordered it to go and, of course, had to wait by the bar for our food. Everyone around us was drinking while we nursed our ice waters. After years of betrayal, I developed a keen sense of focus, which is just another way to say I can become hypervigilant, or really just paranoid. I watched Heidi closely. Anything off in her words, facial mannerisms, body language, speed of talk, alerted me Heidi is about to drink and I have to stop her.

After a while, Heidi got up to use the restroom. *What is she up to? What's she going to try?* If Heidi was to change, so was I. I had to let policing go. My job was not to control her or foil her plans any longer. I was to entrust her to God and endure whatever He's asking me to endure. My job was not to be her conscience or sobriety monitor. If she would drink, we would start over and I'd be there to love her and help her pick up the pieces to rebuild a better and stronger Heidi.

I flat out asked her after she returned from the restroom, "Does sitting here make you want to drink?"

"No," she replied convincingly.

I didn't pick up on any tells that would alert me to her lying. The fear and anxiety that began in the Mirage about her recovery being a desert mirage that would break down after returning to Oklahoma went down a notch. I thought that maybe she had changed for good. Maybe rehab did work. In my mind, it had to work. For the sake of my ministry, my career, and our future it had to work. No church will ever keep a pastor, let alone hire a lead pastor whose wife is so dangerously unpredictable and impulsive. This may have worked. Now we just needed time to heal and rebuild some broken relationships back home. It would all work out.

CHRISTMAS BREAK

The holidays are hard for those who struggle with mood and personality disorders. Alcohol is usually a part of celebrations which makes it even more difficult if there are co-occurring disorders. The Christmas season probably more difficult than most. We typically think of Christmas nostalgically, with the music and carols, the classics on TV, and the trees and lights around town. I nostalgically remember loving Christmas break as a child. I didn't have to worry about school or homework. I would watch Christmas movies feeling safe and comfortable, flanked by the gentle lights of the Christmas tree and kept company by the warm, soft glow of the fireplace. Christmas is usually remembered by most as a happy and exciting time, when everyone seems to be a little bit kinder to one another and a little bit more full of cheer.

However, for many, not just those who suffer from mood and personality disorders, Christmas can be a time that breaks people. It can be a very depressing time of the year. That nostalgia of Christmas can also act as a saddening reminder of what's been lost in the past. People miss loved ones who have passed away and are no longer here to celebrate. Traditions are lost over time and longed for. Some have lost jobs. Others have lost out on love with the ending of a relationship. All this to say, Christmas can be difficult and full of disappointment for many, including Heidi. "The enemy uses disappointments to cause so much trouble in an unsettled heart. A heart hungry for something to ease the ache of disappointment is especially susceptible to the most dangerous forms of desire."[23]

The day we drove back into town was a cold and damp day. The moisture held in the air with the kind of thickness that slowly accumulates without falling. The grey sky spread over us like a heavy blanket concealing us from the sun's sight. It was the absolute opposite of Arizona just the day before. I drove the Mirage to drop off at the car rental with Heidi following. Driving, I glanced back in my rearview mirror; my view of Heidi was obscured by the thin layer of dirty mist being kicked up from the rear tires. My hope for Heidi's recovery was slowly becoming just as obscured as my view of her. The happy laughter and banter of the past week together in the Arizona sunshine felt completely cloaked now by Oklahoma's low hanging sky. Everything felt gloomy, and it wasn't just the weather. I knew her assimilating back in her old environment would be hard, but we both underestimated just how hard it would be.

Heidi came back with a plan she had worked up with her counselor and others back in Arizona. I was a part of this recovery plan and knew from Family Week the signs and behavior that would proceed a relapse if it was to happen. The problem was while Heidi was in rehab they missed diagnosing her BPD altogether. The controlled, lush, and stress free environment of the oasis was free from her everyday triggers. This practically put Heidi's BPD traits in hibernation. Since her traits were hidden, the best they could diagnosis Heidi was with the most apparent, alcoholism and depression. At first glance it seemed to fit but it also didn't account for so much.

At this point, Heidi was willing to do anything for her recovery except Alcoholics Anonymous. There was no way Heidi was going to park her car outside AA for the other moms to see as they drove by with their perfect families. She was not going to subject herself to that open shame and contempt from others. She wasn't going to subjugate herself to the cacophony of her own shame either.

Instead, she opted to do Celebrate Recovery, a Christian twelve-step program. A major problem was that Celebrate Recovery took off for Christmas break and wouldn't meet again until the first Monday after the New Year. Much of her recovery plan would have to wait two weeks, which was not good. All momentum from Arizona seemed to be slowly coming to a halt.

With Christmas just around the corner and Heidi having been gone in Arizona the past month, she was behind on Christmas shopping. She needed to run downtown to do some shopping. This ignited my anxiety; she needed to have my full confidence but I was reluctant, especially after seeing her struggle to assimilate back home. Me controlling her, though, would make things worse. So off she went. She checked in periodically so I could hear her voice and put my anxiety somewhat at ease for a few minutes.

Then it came. The call, but it wasn't Heidi on the other end. It was that old, slow, haunting voice. I knew she had consumed something, but I didn't know what. She grew worse. The slurring. The inability to focus or follow what I was asking her to do. Then came the silence. No more picking up the phone. No more responding to texts. I called my mom and she raced over to watch the kids then I raced downtown.

Our downtown is a typical historic-looking Oklahoma downtown. It is small and quaint, decorated for Christmas this time of year. The street lamps are spun in garland and crowned with wreaths. Christmas lights ornate trees and trim tops of buildings. The street and sidewalks are busier than usual from the invading seasonal shoppers as I make my way slowly up Main Street. I scan the right side of the street, then the left and back to the right for her. Then I spot her at the last block from the end. She is in front of her car, slowly and gracelessly fumbling through her purse. I find a spot to park then anxiously walk over to her. Thankfully, she had lost her key. I had the spare on me so I loaded her up first, then the gifts in the back. I reverse out of the parking space, worried and wondering who all saw her freshly back from rehab already back to old ways. I turned the car toward home.

On the drive back, I lost it. I was angry. I was scared. I was devastated. I was heartbroken. I was yelling. I knew relapse was a thing and a part of recovery, but so soon? The Heidi that I had just found over a week ago in Arizona had been viciously swiped from me once again. The Heidi I had been so excited and thrilled to meet again was gone at that moment. Taking her place in the passenger seat sat that repulsive stranger I hated so much. Hope and healing never felt so impossible. Hope felt like an illusion. Hurting is one thing, but hurting without hope is altogether a completely devastating thing. It all felt like a broken-down desert mirage.

HOPE FOR WHEN YOU CAN'T GET YOUR HOPES UP

A year or so ago, Heidi and I were plopped on the couch one evening watching NBC's *Blue Bloods*. I was on autopilot as the episode mindlessly drifted along until Anthony Abetemarco, ADA Reagan's personal investigator, asked the son of an addict father, "Can you hope without getting your hopes up?"[24] The bizarre question snapped me out of my mindless coasting because I had been thinking a lot about hope recently. I thought about it longer than the writers of the show probably wanted me to, but I really wondered, *Can you hope without getting your hopes up?* What does that even mean? The more I thought about it for me, the question morphed into *Do I still have hope when I can't get my hopes up? Can I have hope when all I seem to feel is disappointment?* The answer I came up with was not just yes, and you must.

We hope day-in and day-out for relief here, answered prayer there, but we are often met with disappointment. The relief doesn't seem to come soon enough. We hope for the next doctor's visit to provide good news. We hope next week will bring a much-needed reprieve. These hopes do not always materialize, leaving us disappointed and—worse—discouraged. Can we, in the midst of what we are suffering, continue to have hope when it feels like we can never catch a break? Can we hope when it is so hard to get our hopes up because we've been let down and disappointed so many times?

Anyone who has ever suffered on any level knows the feeling of disappointment; we get our hopes up only to be let down. We tell ourselves things like "Maybe this will be the job! Maybe now he will come back to his family. Maybe now he will finally stop drinking. Maybe now my child will appreciate me. Maybe now I can get a nap!" Time after time, we get crushed after getting our hopes up, only to have them not materialize. We get our hopes up, believing healing is right around the corner, only to be left disappointed and then discouraged. Hope and healing often seem to elude us like a mirage, and when they do, it is really hard to get our hopes up the next time around. This doesn't mean, however, we do not have hope.

As believers, we have a hope that rises above the tide of disappointment that can pull us down so low. We share a hope that one day death will die and our hurt will be once and for all healed. We will be made whole—mind, body, and soul. Death will no longer touch us, and suffering will no longer stalk us. There will be no disease that can cast disappointment upon us; there will be no heartbreak that will hurt us. On that day, we will finally be conformed to the image of Jesus, who is the image of the invisible God. On that day, everything wrong will be made right and sin and death will lose their hold over us. This hope is what comforts us in our confusion. This hope is what pulls us through our darkest days. So how does this hope, which seems so distant in times of trouble, help us now?

Simply put, our hope is the present enjoyment or the joy we experience when thinking about the sureness of a future promise. Hebrews 6:19-20 tells us that our hope is an anchor that is fastened securely in heaven, extending from Jesus presently in the heavenly temple fastened all the way to our soul. Our hope is sure and steadfast as an anchor because our hope is Jesus Himself. Instead of thinking of a ship anchored downward in a storm, think of your soul being anchored upward—heavenward. No matter how hard life slams against you, no matter how tired you are of taking one relentless wave of discouragement after another, no matter how violently you are tossed emotionally back and forth, you are securely fastened to the one who will never let you go. Like anchors hidden in the deep, our anchor has gone as a forerunner for us, hidden in heaven, having become a high priest forever. Never to exit or vacate His position.

In the Old Testament, the high priest only entered the holiest part of the temple, behind the veil, once a year on the day of atonement, Yom Kippur. Behind the veil was where the holy presence of God dwelt and where the high priest would make atonement for the sins of Israel, then he would make his exit. It was so holy that they fastened a rope to the priest extending out to the others so if things went sideways in there, and the holiness of God killed the priest, they would be able to pull his body out through the veil.

We too are fastened securely to our high priest, who is our hope, not so we can pull Him out if things go sideways, but so that He can pull us through when life becomes just too overwhelming. We may be tossed one side to the other; we may be moved up and down, pushed, and pummeled but our hope in Jesus always pulls us through the storm.

If we lose sight of this hope, our anchor, we give discouragement the power to level our perseverance by distracting us away from the hope that strengthens us. The same hope that pulls us through our present disappointments. When we unfix our eyes from our hope, discouragement will twist how we view the goodness of God, and so begin to warp our view of the One we hope in. It will bring our high and lofty view of God down low.

Our hope is, and always remains, steadfast and sure. However, if we lose our eternal perspective because of our present circumstances, we can easily begin to doubt God and so doubt the sure steadfastness of our hope. Hopelessness then sets in as we take our eyes off, not just the spiritual payout that comes from enduring our suffering, but when we take our eyes off Jesus Himself. This happens so often when we take our eyes off our hope and fasten them on what feels like the permanence of the catastrophe of our circumstances.

Paul reminded his Roman readers of his eternal perspective focused on the truth that what God has in store for us is infinitely more than the instant relief we crave in our suffering. "For I consider that the sufferings of this present time are not worthy to be compared with the glory that is to be revealed to us" (Romans 8:18 NASB). And again he writes,

> For momentary, light affliction is producing for us an eternal weight of glory far beyond all

comparison, while we look not at the things which are seen, but at the things which are not seen; for the things which are seen are temporal, but the things which are not seen are eternal. (2 Corinthians 4:17-18 NASB)

By setting our minds on the things above, by setting our hope in the things that are promised to come to us from heaven, our faith is strengthened. Our disappointments, though constant and annoying, are not worthy to be compared with what God has coming for us. It is perfectly okay to be disappointed, it drives us to dependence on our high priest. Yet, to let disappointment lead us into discouragement will make obsolete from our minds for that which we are enduring. We can't allow disappointment to direct our attention towards earth's continual letdowns, but rather use it as a reminder of our sure and steadfast hope in Jesus. Joni Eareckson Tada put it this way:

When heaven has our attention, a fervid anticipation for God's ultimate reality—appearing with him in glory—begins to glow, making everything earthly pale in comparison. Earth's pain keeps crushing our hopes, reminding us this world can never satisfy; only heaven can.[25]

As disappointment drives us more and more into desperate dependence on Jesus, not only do we see more confidently our hope—our "ultimate reality" which is to come—we also begin to discover the unforeseen joy that comes when we trust God and continue to endure when it seems impossible.

So, can we have hope when it is so hard to get our hopes up? Can we have hope when we are met with what feels like constant disappointment, setbacks, and discouragement? The answer is, yes, we can. Being radically altered by God means pushing past earth's disappointments and setbacks with the steadfast and sure hope that we are eternally fastened to Jesus, the one who promises better things to come and strength in the meantime. Our attention moves from things "hoped" for now, but not guaranteed, to things promised to come. It is knowing that He, our hope and nothing else, is pulling us through the dismal disappointment of earth's continual letdowns. It is this knowledge, this stubborn confidence in our future hope, that we find our present joy.

For many of you, you've been pushing and clawing and still, you have not found this joy. You know you are fastened to your hope but this hope, though steadfast and sure, seems so out of reach and remote you can hardly see what it has to do with today.

When this happens; when disappointment feels as if it is drying us out and depleting our hope, how do we allow it to drive us to a greater dependency on our anchor, Jesus, rather than nosedive us into discouragement? How do we find the strength of hope to keep pushing through earth's disappointments, which can so easily plunder us of our "fervid anticipation for God's ultimate reality"? How do we overcome this same discouragement that has so effortlessly sounded the death knell to the faith of so many before us? When the heat of our suffering is on, discouragement is her warm friend that suffocates the life out of us. So how will we find the strength of hope to persevere and push through the heat of our suffering? We become drought resistant.

DROUGHT RESISTANT

A few years back, I was teaching through Jeremiah's confessions on Wednesday nights at our college gatherings. In Jeremiah's confessions, we find the deep sadness and exhaustion he endured living out his calling. We see him, more than any other prophet, feeling dried out and depleted. The confessions show us the raw reality of obeying the call of God to suffer. Jeremiah, more than others, has taught me how to find the strength of hope when all we do is hurt with a hurt draped in discouragement. He has taught me how to let God mature my faith when I feel mastered by fear. We will all, at some time or another, feel as if we have run aground and wonder, *What's the point anymore?* Jeremiah teaches us the key to persevering is not about having a point, but about having a nourished faith.

When the heat turns up on us, whether it be an addiction, loss of a loved one, depression, loss of a career, cancer diagnosis, a birth defect of a child, or a cheating spouse, we all have to be ready to respond. During these times when we feel the heaviness of discouragement's suffocating effects, we will be tempted to throw in the sweat-drenched towel on God. There will be times when hope really does seem to elude us. It feels like our hope is just a cruel mirage that vanishes once within our grasp. But once our sense of hope is lost so is the chance of us being radically altered by God. When Jesus calls us to follow Him to places we don't want to go, and while on the journey we are depleted by discouragement, Jeremiah helps us find the strength of hope to flourish, by teaching us how to keep our faith nourished.

In chapter 17, Jeremiah teaches a crucial principle for when the heat of our suffering turns up. The principle is this: the person who trusts in their own power, turning away from God during difficult times, dries out. On the other hand, the one who trusts in God's ability to strengthen them will become the one who is drought resistant. Unlike the people of Judah during Jeremiah's day, we want to be people who, when the heat is on and we just can't catch a break, continue to trust in our God. To illustrate how we continue to trust God, Jeremiah writes in verses 7–8 that the one who trusts in the Lord will be like a tree planted by water, which extends his roots by the stream. This person does not fear when the heat is turned on, and his leaves do not wither when beat down by the scorching desert sun, but the leaves will maintain its green. This person maintains his life because he has entrusted it to the only source of life in the desert—the living water (Jeremiah 17:13).

If you are starting to believe hope and healing is nothing more than a desert mirage, and bouts of discouragement have your prayers looking more like doubts, then it is time to desperately extend the roots of your faith. When the heat of your suffering is sucking the life out of you, you have to start daily tapping into the only source there is for life, Jesus.

In John 4, Jesus declares Himself the living water which truly satisfies. Jesus is not just the source for satisfying our thirst for receiving eternal life. As the living water, He is also the source for satisfying our thirst to *experience* daily that eternal life we already possess. It is by grace through faith we maintain our constant connection with the source that sustains our new life. John called this connection *abiding*. The word abide means to make your home. Where you live is where you abide. We crave eternal life, and Jesus is the one who gives this life, not only to have forever but to experience today. We experience this life—not just unendingly but also abundantly—when we make Him the home of our faith and hope. The longer the roots of our faith abide or make Him and His love our home, the more we experience His joy being made more and more full in us (John 15:11). As we look to Jesus to be the source of our satisfaction and not our circumstances, we become strangely satisfied in a way that is unforeseen.

Some days, the roots of your faith will bathe in the stream, and other days, you will feel like you are desperately extending to the water with all you have, begging for just a drip. Those days it will feel like the water purposely meanders around your roots, but it does not. You are still connecting and abiding; you are still growing. You will get the shot of the hydration you need at just the right time. There is nothing better you can do for yourself than to continually be stretching out the roots of your faith to the source of life that keeps you green and thriving when the heat is on. In times of suffering, surviving is about adapting but thriving is about abiding.

By waking up early every morning to extend the roots of my faith in prayer and meditation on God's word, He not only kept me alive when the heat was on, but He made my faith thrive in the months of drought to come when I needed Him the most. He made me drought resistant and He wants to make you drought resistant also.

Are you in a season of drought? Are you in a wasteland feeling like hope and healing are toying with you? Does hope elude you like a mirage or a meandering stream? Are you experiencing a discouragement that has you spending your time brooding and resenting? Do you catch yourself being ungrateful? Does God feel cruel sometimes? Are you ready to give up? Are you thinking about throwing in your sweat-drenched towel on God? Don't give up on God because healing isn't happening fast enough. Reach. Extend the roots of your faith.

Jeremiah says that the one who doesn't do this; the one who gives up and forsakes God by making the home of his or her faith abide elsewhere dries out. Don't give up on God because discouragement is assaulting your sense of hope; your sense of peace. Reach. Extend. Stretch out with everything you have toward Jesus. If all you have in you right now is to just beg for Him to revive you or to just sustain you, then beg! That's exactly what Jeremiah's faith looked like (17:14-18). It's what my faith has looked like time and time again. I have journals with pages that just read, "Revive me, God! Sustain me." It doesn't seem like much but it is what abiding in faith looks like; continually, day after day, going back to the source of life.

Finding our satisfaction in Jesus, rather than in our circumstances, results not in a weak depleted hope, but a defiant hope. It results in a defiant confidence, a resolute and battle-hardened hope. Jesus, the one who satisfies you will sustain you. Tomorrow will come, and with it, His hope renewing strength for you. Just because God's timing is hard for us to accept, don't let it cause you to extend your confidence away from Him toward the empty cisterns of this world. Sex won't save you. Money and power won't propel you. Food is a fickle comforter and gaming is a relationship thief and an isolation instigator. Whatever you treasure apart from God as your source of life will leave you dried out when the heat is on. Stop desperately trying to tap into empty sources that falsely promise satisfaction during difficult times. Reach for Jesus. When the heat is on and hope for you or your loved one continues to feel like a mirage in the desert, keep extending the roots of your faith to the only true source of life—the living water Himself, Jesus.

CHAPTER 8

It's an Ostrich

T HAT CHRISTMAS FOLLOWING REHAB WAS ROUGH, BUT WE made it through and it was now a new year. As the year turned, I'm desperately hoping for a better year than the last. I realized this wishful thinking had become a routine now with every new year, always hoping the next year would be better than the last. Heidi had gotten back on track with her recovery plan she developed in rehab. That first Monday of the new year we would attend Celebrate Recovery. We drove an hour every Monday for Heidi to meet with her counselor then grab a quick bite to eat before heading over to the CR meeting that evening.

About the time Heidi had started gaining a little momentum in her recovery, the church's Wednesday night activities began to ramp back up for me. I go home that first Wednesday and find Heidi slumped in a chair. The babysitter was upstairs with our son while the twins napped. I helped Heidi come to enough to walk her to the car to take her to my parents' house. She had to leave. I was simply enforcing the boundary we agreed upon.

She can't be around the children. After I settle her in I go back to the church to get youth set up for that night. Heidi sleeps all afternoon and into the evening.

I finished up with the youth and was on my way to campus to teach our college gathering that night. I'm turning the corner, about a mile away from campus, when Heidi calls irate. I explain to her why she's at my mom's and why she can't go home. It was not the best time to remind her of the boundary we agreed upon. She wasn't emotionally in the right place to have that talk. I wasn't either. I was upset. I didn't realize it at the time, but now I know I was only stoking the shame she was unable to manage due to her then undiagnosed BPD. By refusing to come to see her, I was intensifying the self-hate she was trapped in and the overwhelming feeling of abandonment all borderlines dread. I tell her we will talk after I finish on campus around 10:00 that night. She tells me not to bother; she has already cut her wrist and hangs up the phone.

FOLLOW THE LIGHT

I immediately call her back. No answer. I've already flipped a U-turn for my parents' home and I'm flying. My anxious grip frantically twists back and forth around the steering wheel. I'm panicked because months earlier Heidi had befriended a girl in rehab who was a cutter. Heidi had told me this particular girl explained to her the way to cut yourself if you wanted to go fast. As soon as Heidi told me she cut her wrist, that conversation sprung to the forefront of my mind. Eighty percent of those who suffer from BPD have suicidal tendencies. Ten percent of those actually follow through with the suicide. I wasn't going to get to her fast enough, so I called my dad, who was at my house helping my mom with the children.

"Hello." He answered.

"Dad! Get home! Heidi cut her wrist!" Click.

As soon as I hang up with my dad, I call 911 and tell them what's going on while I'm driving like a tactile missile toward the house. I make a left turn and floor it. Then a right and I punch the gas once again. I ramp up over a hill and see off in the dark distance ahead of me lights. They are the lights of a fire engine. I know exactly where they are going. They are headed for Heidi. I follow the flashing red light ahead of me. Soon I catch up to the light. Now I'm stuck behind the light. This big fire engine is taking up the whole neighborhood street. The dimly lit neighborhood, full of twists and turns, is making it difficult for them to find the house. The light I chased after is now slowing me down and seems to be lost.

As the truck finally pulls in front of my parents' home, I get around it and enter the left side of the circle drive while the truck takes the right. We all arrive at the same time. Fire engine, police, and unmarked police. The emergency lights, all delicately dancing off the surrounding homes, looked like Christmas had come early. I ran into my parents' home then into their bedroom to find Heidi sitting up in the bed. Firefighters and police, both, pour through the front door after me. As the room fills with emergency responders, Heidi begins to cry uncontrollably.

The drive to Heidi that night was tormenting. Would I find Heidi dead? Would everything we've been through have all been for nothing? Had our suffering been meaningless only to end in death? What would I tell our three children? As I drove that night

I couldn't get to her soon enough, and to make it worse, I got slowed down by the very fire engine headed to save her.

There is a similar story to this in the gospels. A father comes to Jesus and pleads for Him to come heal his twelve-year-old daughter. Time is running out. She is dying. Jesus gets off the boat and is immediately met by this father along with countless others. Jesus agrees to go with the father. The crowd, however, was too thick to move quickly. The crowd pressed in on Him from every side.

When Jesus's boat made landfall, I think it must have looked like when the Beatles landed in America. The crowd was crazy. Jesus was a rock star. I'm sure, as desperate as the father was, Jesus wasn't moving fast enough for him. This man couldn't get Jesus to his daughter fast enough. Not long after this father gets Jesus moving toward his daughter, Jesus stops because someone touches him.

Jesus stops and asks, "Who touched me?" A seemingly puzzling question since the crowd was on top of Him, as well as His disciples. Peter, probably a bit confused by Jesus's question, asks a question of his own. "What do you mean? Everyone is touching you, the crowd is all over us." No doubt the father had to wonder why Jesus wasn't sharing his anxiety or his urgency as his daughter is dying. I bet this father was mystified that Jesus could care more about being touched in a crowd than extending a saving touch to his precious little girl.

From the father's perspective, he went to Jesus for an urgent solution, but Jesus seemed to be in no hurry. Sometimes when we choose to follow Jesus, it feels like He doesn't care. Like He's moving too slowly. It feels like He's lost and can't find the house due to the dimly lit neighborhood full of twists and turns. Or, He cares more about someone touching His cloak than extending His healing touch to our pain.

Then, in the story, unable to escape notice the culprit who had touched Jesus steps forward through the crowd. It's none other than *her*, the unclean woman who had been hemorrhaging blood for the past twelve years. Everyone knew of her defiled touch. She was the town's lost cause. No one touched her, and everyone knew not to get close enough to be touched by her. She had been to every doctor in town seeking a cure to help her get clean again, but no one could help her. As a result of her being ritually unclean, she was banished to the fringe of society, forgotten to die. You can picture it as the crowd gasps and shrieks. In one sudden movement, all together, the crowd fans out in a circle formation around this woman, leaving her exposed and isolated in the middle. Open to shame. Open to humiliation. Open to judgment. She is unable to escape Jesus's notice and that of the whole crowd. Everyone moved away but one: Jesus.

Jesus isn't defiled by her touch. Conversely, she has been made clean by His. She explains herself to Jesus and to the crowd (which she has stealthily rubbed shoulders). She explained how the moment she touched Jesus, she was healed. The crowd with skepticism thinks she's lying. Then Jesus looks at her and calls her "Daughter." This is the only place in all of the gospels where Jesus addresses an individual directly as His *daughter*. I believe Jesus calls her His daughter purposely within earshot of the desperate father whose own daughter lies dying. "Daughter, your faith has healed you." You can't miss it. Jesus saves daughters.

That very moment the news came to Jairus, the father, that his daughter had indeed died. Why the pitstop? Why the delay?

Jesus thought healing a woman suffering from a twelve-year-old hemorrhage was more important than saving a twelve-year-old girl's life?

The thing is, Jesus knew Jairus's daughter had already died when He stopped. The devasting news was moments away from being delivered to Jairus, and this is why Jesus stopped. This is why Jesus seemed to delay. He knew Jairus was about to be handed the heart-crushing, life-altering news. Jesus wasn't being cruel by not sharing this father's urgency. Jesus loved this father and didn't want his faith to fail at the overwhelming news of the loss of his daughter.

This is why Jesus stopped. Jesus drew attention to this lost cause of a daughter in the crowd—this incurable woman that only He could heal. By Jesus strategically delaying, He had a plan to build Jairus's faith to endure the tragic news of his own daughter's death. In this act Jesus was telling Jairus, "I know how to save daughters. Trust Me." Jesus was giving Jairus something to believe so when the crisis of faith came upon him, he could take Jesus's word to heart, which was, "Do not be afraid *any longer*; only believe, and she will be made well" (Luke 8:50 NASB).

It's not easy to follow the Light when He seems to not care or is taking His sweet time. You pray and pray and beg and plead, and sometimes it feels like He is lost on His way to answering you. Sometimes it feels like He's not even hearing you. He does. He's there. He's not delaying, no one is slowing Him down, and His timing is perfect, even though we feel like our time is running out. This waiting may be Him preparing you or Him training you because sometimes it gets worse before it gets better. Perhaps He is building your faith so it won't fail in the long run. Can you imagine what Jairus felt when he heard the devastating words "Your daughter has died"? How much more traumatizing if Jesus hadn't just demonstrated to Jairus that He alone can save daughters? He alone can do what we cannot. He alone can save the lost causes.

Before Jesus tells Jairus to believe, Jesus gave Jairus something to believe in: He saves daughters. This story gives you something to believe in as well. Don't stop following the Light when He appears lost or when you feel like He doesn't share your urgency. He does. He hears you, and He is preparing you. He's maturing your faith and radically altering you. God isn't afraid of how reckless things appear. They are still very much in His control. We shouldn't be afraid either when God Himself appears reckless because He is still very much in control. Our God is not afraid to get real with us, to get raw with us, if it is what it takes to alter us. When He does get raw, like Jairus, *believe.*

RIGHTEOUS BUT RAW GOD

A week after chasing the light comes Hero Day at our son's school. I go pick up our lunch and cry while I listen to Jimmy Eat World's "Drugs or Me." I'm crushed. I'm trying to follow Jesus, but I can't see Him working. I can't feel His presence. I know our situation is going to get worse before it gets better, but it seems like whatever "worse" is, I can't bear it. Where is God's urgency? Can't He see we're dying?

How do we faithfully follow Jesus when He isn't moving fast enough for our liking? The answer is in the word *faithfully.* We are frustrated with Jesus when He seems to delay because we are scared or anxious. We know our own powerlessness to take control and fix the situation. Fear and doubt replace faithful remembrance that He has already given us something, like He did for Jairus, to believe. When it feels like He doesn't share our urgency, we are tempted to urgently look for a quicker solution other than Him. A different source of life. We wait and wait for Him to show up and save the day. We wait for Him to bring resolution to our suffering (or at least a good answer that gives us meaning in the suffering) and His presence is absent—so it feels. Your world is falling apart and your loved one is dying before your eyes, and where is Jesus? Does He not see everything is out of control?

Heidi is seventeen days sober, the longest ever outside of rehab and her pregnancies. We never counted days until after rehab. I was never really keen on counting because I knew if Heidi got a lot of days under her belt and had to start over, she would have a major crash into depression and want to give up altogether. Starting over would seem pointless to her, and healing would feel impossible to me.

The sun is shining; it is a warm February morning. We had some returns to make. Everything seemed fine that day. On our way to the store, I trusted her to go in to make the returns on the condition she brought back the gift card and receipt. She does. All is well. Then, minutes later, as we travel down the road, she changes. Her demeanor alters. She becomes drowsy and thick tongued, slurring her words. She split the return onto two gift cards, giving me one with its receipt and using the other.

Later, when she becomes lucid, depression deluges her. An avalanche of self-hate and hopelessness buries her. She burrows deep into our bedding as if she knows of some dark hole there where she could lose herself. She buries herself in her grave of pillows, one pillow stacked on top of another. The bed's wooden headboard an unmarked tombstone. This is the closest she can come to suicide, an alternative death with which she punishes herself. She feels she doesn't deserve to live so she seals herself in a tomb of darkness; a mausoleum of loneliness. She doesn't know why she drinks when she doesn't want to. If she can't trust her own thoughts, what can she trust? How can she live if she can't believe her own inner voice? How can she trust herself if she is self-deceiving? Betrayed by her own thoughts, it all feels hopeless. For both her and me.

The shame spins Heidi out. She puts together a streak of impressive, but not surprising, days of finding ways to secretly drink to punish herself and kill the shame overtaking her, all at once. I'm losing it watching her lose it. I don't know what to do anymore. She's not going back to rehab. She doesn't want to follow her recovery plan. The only thing I can think of is to rework my boundaries and communicate them better. My journal during these days is page after page of the same prayer as I read through Psalm 119. "Revive me!"

It is a dark, cold morning. I wake up once again before everyone and head to Heidi's office. I softly close the double doors behind me. Her office window is cracked so cold air seeps in, gliding over the window seal, cascading down onto the wood floor. The cold air pools under the desk I sit, adjacent to the window. I wrap myself in a blanket and open my Bible to Job. Job 38 is one of my favorite passages. We see a lot of rawness from Job, but in Job 38–42, we see a righteous but raw God. God comes to Job in a violent and, I'm sure, terrifying whirlwind. His coming to Job and His message reveals God's rawness as He gets very real about who He is and how He reserves the right to do as

He wishes. A section that stood out to me that I had always just read past is the following from Job:

> The ostriches' wings flap joyously
> With the pinion and plumage of love,
> For she abandons her eggs to the earth
> And warms them in the dust,
> And she forgets that a foot may crush them,
> Or that a wild beast may trample them.
> She treats her young cruelly, as if *they* were not hers;
> Though her labor be in vain, *she* is unconcerned;
> Because God has made her forget wisdom,
> And has not given her a share of understanding.
> (Job 39:13–17 NASB)

The ostrich in these verses sounded like Heidi. Heidi's brain seemed to have been rewired as a result of BPD to forget understanding. The apparent disengagement of Heidi's stop system of her brain resulted in her reckless behavior. She was living recklessly as if she had lost all wisdom and understanding. God speaks of the ostrich to make His point that even though the ostrich may look reckless, her recklessness is not apart from God's sovereign control. In other words, God doesn't look at the ostrich and think, *Well, that one backfired on me. I don't know why she appears so out of control. She's broke. Oh well. I'll do better next time.* The apparent recklessness of the ostrich is no surprise to Him, and her behavior is not apart from His sovereign purposes.

Reading this revives me. Even though everything was apparently out of control and reckless, none of it was apart from God. I was comforted by His control. If Heidi has indeed lost

wisdom and understanding, it's *because God has made her forget.*
He's still in control. None of this was happening without His
approval, and this truth strengthened me to have the confidence
to keep going.

I didn't have my journal with me, and I didn't want to get up
because I was snug in the blanket, so I grabbed a scratch piece
of paper that sat on Heidi's desk and wrote down what I was
thinking.

February 7,

Job 39:13–17
Like the ostrich, You've made Heidi forget wisdom
and You have not given her understanding. She
abandons her children where they can be hurt.
She labors in vain, and she has no healthy fear,
but none of what the ostrich does is apart from
You, God.

When she hurts me, help me look at Heidi and
not get depressed or mad but see You (working)
as hard as it may be. Will Your awesome power,
which commands the waves and the light each
morning to take hold of the ends of the earth,
empower me to surrender to You even when it
doesn't make sense? Will Your grace sustain me
one more day? I need You today. "Every hour, I
need you."

Application
Because I exist for You, God, today I will accept Heidi's lies because she cannot lie to me without Your purposes being behind her. Somehow her deception and self-destruction accomplish Your purposes and plan. It is too far beyond me to understand, but I believe in You.

Later that day, Heidi comes walking out of her office while holding a piece of scratch paper up by her head. "So I'm an ostrich?" She was not too happy. No woman wants her husband to describe her as an ostrich. Perhaps an elegant swan or something a bit more graceful, but not a dirty, round-bodied, long-neck, skinny-legged, grumpy-faced ostrich.

We are to follow Jesus, the Light, even when we feel He doesn't share our urgency; even when He feels absent. We are to listen to God when He gets raw with us because it is in these times He is telling us something to build our faith so it doesn't fail when things get worse. And sometimes they do get worse. Two things God taught me during this time were, first, to stop living as if God exists for me. God doesn't exist for my dream life. He created me for Him. And second, God convinced me during this time that nothing happens apart from His plan. I believe God is good. Not good like a really good burger. Not good like a really good movie or friend. God is good in a way we can't even fully comprehend, but in a way we can fully be comforted.

We lack His eternal and omniscient vantage point. So most of the time—really more like all the time—we lack His full reasoning for allowing things to appear and feel so awful. I clearly do not know all His reasons, but I do know one of His good reasons that He calls us to follow Him into suffering. It is so that our life would be radically altered into looking like His Son's life. His Son, whom the Bible describes as despised and forsaken of men, a man of sorrows and acquainted with grief. Beaten. Scourged. Speared. Nailed. These are just a few physical sufferings, but what about the emotional? Abandoned by His closest friends the hour He needed them most. Shamed. Isolated. Rejected by His own people. He was anxious to the point of sweating blood. Depressed. Intimidated. Threatened. Last, but not least, He was tormented by the devil himself.

Peter writes in his first letter, "For you have been called for this purpose, since Christ also suffered for you, leaving you an example for you to follow in His steps" (1 Peter 2:21 NASB). God doesn't just allow suffering to enter our life. He has called us into it. He has called us to follow His Son's example to entrust ourselves to God and endure. He has called us to be like Him.

Sometimes things get worse before they get better. God is not afraid to get raw with us, to flex His majestic muscles to mature our faith. The ostrich is our reminder that when God is getting raw with us and things look completely out of control, the truth is that nothing is happening apart from Him. He is righteous. He's got this.

GOD WORKS LATE ON VALENTINE'S

I felt different. Confident. Not confident in myself but in God. I knew He was sovereign, and I knew He was working all things, but something clicked in me. My wife was an ostrich and all the hurt she was causing me was taken away at that moment. All the hurt I anticipated could be caused to me was also taken away.

There came a sense of meaning behind the madness. Whatever she did, and whatever reckless behavior I saw, I knew somehow it was not apart from God. It all was one piece of the grand plan.

Heidi was still in CR and trying to find a sponsor. She had found a potential sponsor, but for this woman to agree to sponsor, Heidi would first have to complete ninety in ninety. Typically this means ninety AA meetings in ninety days. As mentioned earlier, CR was different than AA and would allow for church and Bible studies to count as meetings. Heidi, still not broken in her pride, reluctantly agreed. She wasn't looking for recovery at this point; she was looking to check things off a list. Sunday rolled around. She went to church that morning then reluctantly an AA meeting that afternoon. Following that meeting, we went to a church that had a 4:00 p.m. service. After that, she would then meet me at our church for our youth Bible study.

That evening, our church sat empty and quiet. A youth strolled in, then another, and another. It was a low turnout, but we had some kids out of town and, after all, it was a Sunday night. The lesson was a short one. As I sat there teaching my mind was not quiet. An anxious thought strolled in, then another, and another. My breathing grew shallow and stiff. Heidi never showed up.

I was just about to finish up when my phone alerted me that Heidi had arrived at the church. Her tardiness had me troubled. I had, once more, the swirling emotions of gratefulness that she was safe and an alarming apprehensiveness that she's been altered. I paused the lesson and went to the other side of the building where she would park by my office. She gets out and I can tell she's consumed something mood altering. She can't drive home, so I bring her into my office to conceal her from the youth. I sit her in my office chair, then go back out to the Bible study. Once back at the study I notice we are now missing a girl. I go back toward my office and from down the hall, I can see her through the office windows. She's talking to Heidi. I go in and tell her we're finishing the lesson. It's too late. A youth under my watch has been exposed to my inebriated wife. We finish the lesson. Slowly, a youth strolls out the door, then another, and another. Then we leave.

Since I work on Sunday I had Monday off. That next day she and I both know the cameras at the church caught her altered the day before. We also know the cameras caught her the week before taking hand sanitizer out of a nursery room during a youth event. The cameras didn't catch me catching her though. It doesn't matter. Tuesday comes. I go into the office and sit at my desk. Everything was normal except for the whispering, "Does she not think we can see her?" The camera feeds are viewable on the computers and phones. They are most likely talking about Heidi. Then I hear more whispers. I'm almost certain it is about Heidi and me now, but I don't know for sure. Everyone is talking but no one is talking to me so I keep working. That afternoon I get a call. Heidi did it again. I go home and get her. I take her to her parents' home an hour away this time. She can no longer stay at our home in this state. She says she wants recovery, but she's relapsing. Nothing is indicating to me she wants to stop or even knows how to stop. She goes to live with her parents until she gets serious.

When Heidi and I were dating, I made the hour drive to where she went to school for our first Valentine's. I picked up sushi from the restaurant we went to on our second first date. I put the sushi on ice in the cooler. I strategically positioned the flowers where they would not fall during the drive. I bought a movie called *Trapped in Paradise* as a fun gift since months earlier we had gotten trapped in Crested Butte, Colorado due to heavy snow. Valentine's has always been for us a special, but not hyped, holiday. We always stay low-key. Usually, we cook a crazy, big Valentine dinner together: steak, lobster, fried pickles, zucchini—whatever we want. I will say, however, on our third Valentine's Day while still in Dallas, I got out of class and bought a ton of candles from a dollar store around the corner. I spent the afternoon cleaning the apartment and setting flower petals and candles for when she arrived home from work. I definitely peaked that Valentine's.

Except for my overly ambitious flower petal Valentine's, the day historically for us has never been a big deal with high expectations. The only expectation is being together. Wednesday is Valentine's and I want her home. However, she doesn't want to come home. I don't remember if she was mad at me or ashamed or both. Now, I know she didn't want to come home, not because she didn't want to, but because of her BPD she wanted me to come get her so she could have a reason to believe I still loved her.

Our phone conversation was painful. She had been to a meeting and picked up another twenty-four-hour chip. I hated counting days. To start counting back at day 1 seemed to perpetuate Heidi's shame/drinking cycle. Enforcing the boundary had been hard. Sticking with the boundary was even harder. She had to be twenty-four hours sober and convince me she is serious about recovery before coming home. I remember being crushed when I heard her say that she didn't know what she wanted anymore. It seemed so obvious to me.

It was hard hearing her not want to be with me on Valentine's.

This would be our first Valentine's apart, ever. No steak, no lobster, no fried whatever. No *Trapped in Paradise*. The only place I was trapped in was my very own personal purgatory. I had not lost my confidence in God though. I knew this relapse, in some inconceivable way, was a part of God's plan and He was still working that Valentine's. I was crushed but still confident. I went to bed early, hoping Thursday would be better. It would not. Although it was going to get worse before it got better, in His raw and righteous way, God was working late on that Valentine's Day to end a dream; a dream that was solely my own and not His for me.

We have to elevate our view of God. We have to practice day after day thinking and living as if God truly is as supreme as we claim Him to be. When God gets raw with us in our suffering, we have to have the courage of faith to face His whirlwind. In His rawness, like with Job, His truth will strengthen us and give us perspective. It doesn't matter how urgent the situation is; God has a plan, and it involves maturing your faith and altering you into someone who looks like His Son.

Sometimes it gets worse before it gets better and He's getting us ready so our faith won't fail as He did with Jairus's faith. If it gets worse before it gets better, remember the ostrich. The ostrich reminds us that nothing happens apart from God. Having a high view of God brings us an enormous amount of peace. No matter how reckless and desperate, no matter how dangerous or devasting, your suffering is not apart from a good God's plan. It's an ostrich. Your suffering is an ostrich; it appears reckless, out of control, and even dangerous, but none of it is apart from God's good plan.

If you are not truly persuaded that God is good regardless of your circumstances and your ostrich is bigger than your God, then it will be nearly impossible for you to experience His peace in your pain and the unforeseen joy He has in store for you. Like Jairus, in the middle of your fear and urgency, Jesus is asking you to believe in Him. Believe He is in control. Believe in His raw and righteous approach. That faith will then open up something so powerful; something no amount of pain or hurt in this world can ever take from you. That something is your worship.

CHAPTER 9

Without Cause

V ALENTINE'S DAY IS OVER WITH THE ARRIVAL OF THURSDAY morning. Heidi gets started on some work she could do from her parents' home. Later that morning, she decides to go to an AA meeting in town. While there, she scores $2 from an attendee and stops by a CVS on the way back. She buys two small bottles of hand sanitizer. She drinks some and becomes nauseated; she throws it up at a nearby gas station, just like I had been praying would happen if she tried to consume that junk. However, not even my answered prayer could stop what God had planned for this day.

She arrives back at her parents' home and calls to tell me how the meeting went. I can tell on the phone she consumed something altering. Heidi goes downhill fast. She becomes drastically altered. Moments later she passes out from the second mini bottle of sanitizer. Later that evening, Heidi agrees to check herself into a facility in the city. All the plans get made and I will meet her at the treatment facility.

That evening, out of answers and out of energy, exhausted, I get in my car to make the hour drive to meet Heidi at the facility where she will be admitting herself. I aim my car eastward; I then charge toward the rising night as the dull sun slowly slipped behind me into a low pocket of dank clouds suspended slightly above earth's end. Night had now advanced when the darkness inside my car cab is interrupted with the soft glow of my cell phone. It is the father of the girl who walked into my office Sunday evening. I answer. Lovingly and graciously, he tells me he and his wife will be pulling their children from the program. I plead with him not to do so. I (and another leader) had been investing in his children, especially his older son, for the last two years. This would be crushing. We were building the whole group around the leadership of his son and a couple others. To take his son out would erase two years of work and stunt the program. I tell him to keep his children in the youth group, and instead, I will leave.

My job was not to just disciple and grow college students, but our church's youth as well, but with youth about to leave, I was having an adverse effect. I realized what I had known for months, which was I could no longer manage my ministry and my marriage. I was losing both that night.

I pulled into the sad and decrepit parking lot where I would meet Heidi. The parking lot was dark, lit slightly by the tired light from inside the treacherous building we were about to enter. The night felt especially dark as well with no moon or stars. Our situation felt the darkest. I arrive before Heidi. While waiting, I send a text to both my boss and the executive pastor. I explain that I was about to check Heidi into another treatment facility and that I would be resigning formally first thing in the morning.

Heidi pulled into the lot, headlights slicing through the night. She parked two spaces to my left. I get out. Heidi gets out. She's been crying and has a look on her face. I know that look. On her face she wore a dejected darkness; a darkness, sadly, I had seen many times now. Derelict and depressed, her countenance hung as we gather her bags and roll of quarters she'll need for phone calls. She tells me she may lose her job. I tell her I've already lost mine. At that moment, it felt like we had nothing except each other. Even that, however, we wouldn't have in just a few moments as we enter the building.

After we talked with the admission counselor, who stayed late for us to come that night, she led us out of her closet office to the right. We made the short walk down a crude corridor back to the main lobby we first met. I hug Heidi and kiss her. Once again, like in Arizona, I look at her and tell her she is courageous for getting help. She then turns her back to me to walk through a dismal looking doorway. As she passes through, with a loud, drawn-out squeak the double doors devour her. I turn and head toward the front where an older witch-like woman, who guarded the plagued facility, sat with translucent hair behind a tortured desk. She looks up at me expressionless. As our eyes meet she turns to hit a single button on the wall to unlock the front door. I walk out of that depressed facility desperately praying this would be the last time I had to leave Heidi in a strange place. I get in my car. I pull out of the lonely parking lot to make the hour drive back home.

Merging onto the highway, I aim my car westward and charge through the night. Once on the road, I called my mom to let her know the latest. It was a quick call. She cried. We hung up and I soon was overwhelmed by all that had just unfolded that evening. I was out of ministry. Heidi was back in treatment.

Healing and hope felt once again like a desert mirage. How do I hope without getting my hopes up? I got my hopes up again only for them to vanish. I begin to pray.

Everything that was happening in my life should have devastated me. The hope I felt back in Arizona was as distant as Arizona itself. I was living what felt like a worst-case scenario. I had to quit my dream of being a pastor and my wife was back in treatment. While my mind is sifting through a million thoughts on the drive home, a song begins to play over the radio. I had just recently heard Hillsong's "So Will I (100 Billion X)" the week before, so it was still new to me. The song comes on while my mind is racing. I'm hearing the lyrics and the repetition of the music playing over and over in the background to my prayer. The song's bridge climbs along with my anxious thoughts and prayers up to God. As my thoughts and prayers crescendo, they do so along with the song.

> If the stars were made to worship, so will I
> If the mountains bow in reverence, so will I
> If the oceans roar Your greatness, so will I
> For if everything exists to lift You high, so will I

As each line from the song builds one on top of the other, and the music with it, my praying gradually climbs and my determination with hopes that Satan (or whichever crony of his) might be listening. I yell, "You can kill my ministry! You can steal my wife! You can destroy even my life, but you can't have my worship!"

(The music continues to rise with its lyrics in the background to my prayer.)

If the wind goes where You send it, so will I
If the rocks cry out in silence, so will I
If the sum of all our praises still falls shy ...

(As the song crescendos, so do I.)

Then we'll sing again a hundred billion times

As the music climaxes and plays out, I feel supernatural. Right then, I felt like I had just kicked the most powerful angelic being in the universe square between the legs. (I know angels don't have reproductive parts, but you get it.) It felt as if Satan reduced my life to rubble and I'm still standing. I didn't break. I had been altered. I refused to surrender my worship to Satan because I had already surrendered myself to God.

Only a person who is being radically altered by the grace of God doesn't back down. I refused to curse God and die. Instead of cursing God, I blessed Him. I may have ended my ministry and my wife may have lost her job. I just left my wife behind for who knows how long in a dark and haunted facility. I don't know where money will come from, and I don't know about insurance for my children. I have no idea what will be said about me personally at the church in the coming days and weeks or months. But I do not care because I was made to worship God regardless of all these things. In that moment, it was as if Satan had given me his best shot and I won; I still worshiped God. Satan can steal my wife. He can ruin my reputation and my ministry. He can rip me of financial security and peace. But he cannot take away my worship! That's mine to give, and I am not giving it up. I am made to worship, and so I will. If suffering causes my worship to still fall shy, then I will sing it again a hundred billion times.

This is what it means to be altered—you worship. Not that you sing worship songs in your car or even church, but you follow Jesus exactly where it is you don't want to go, and when you get there, you continue to worship Him, regardless of the substantial sadness or darkness that may be hoisted upon you. You do this because this is what you were made to do. "Worship is first your identity before it is ever your activity."[26] You and I were made to worship, but often we don't know what we're made of until our suffering reveals it.

Will you still worship in your suffering? Will you bless, or will you curse? Many of us are "worshiping" as an activity without ever realizing worship is our identity—it's who we are. And who we are, does not oscillate as our circumstances shift back and forth from good and bad. Too often, when suffering begins the "worship" ends. Suffering is advantageous to us because it reveals whether or not our worship is merely an activity or a realized part of our identity as disciples.

God will humor Satan with a leash longer than we will ever understand. God will share dominion with Satan. God has granted him to be the god of this age. God has allowed him to roam this earth like a roaring lion. God shares so much with Satan, for whatever reason, but He will never share His worship. Ever. The one thing Satan wants above all, he can't take. He can't steal it. Only we can give it to him. Satan may ruin you. He may assassinate your reputation. He may cause your friends to distance from you, but it's not apart from God's good plan, so you keep worshiping. We must wrap our hearts around the truth that God does not exist for our happiness. In doing so, our worship will then always be in response to who God is, regardless of whatever our circumstances may be. We don't worship God because we believe His existence necessitates our happiness. We worship God because we believe His existence necessitates our worship. And this worship is without cause.

TORN AND HUMBLED HEART

This is not some mysterious truth that I stumbled upon. This is the book of Job. When people find themselves in difficult times or times of tremendous undeserved suffering, often they turn to the book of Job. Most turn to the book of Job looking for the answer as to *why* we suffer—more specifically, *why they* are suffering. God never addresses why we suffer or why He allows us to suffer in the book of Job. What we see is that God allows Job to suffer unjustly or without cause, so we may learn *how* we too are to suffer in view of *who* God is. So, ultimately, we don't need to know why we suffer; we just need to know God. Job is one of the oldest books in the Bible, and in it, one of the oldest truths is found. God does not exist for our happiness; we exist for His glory. We exist to bless God, not be blessed by God.

We find in chapter 1 that Satan shows up before the throne of God on some special day when all the "sons of God" (angelic beings) come and present themselves before Him. Satan, an angelic being, is naturally present. God asks Satan what he's been doing, to which Satan replies that he's just been roaming the earth. Not sure what God is thinking next, it sounds a lot like He's trolling Satan, deliberately trying to provoke him and work him up about Job. He asks Satan if he has considered His servant Job. He describes Job as a one of a kind on earth, "a blameless and upright man, fearing God and turning away from evil" (Job 1:8 NASB). Satan comes back at God with a question, an accusation, and a challenge. "Does Job fear God for nothing?" (Job 1:9 NASB). Satan's question is merely a setup for the accusation he disguises as another question. "Have You not made a hedge about him and his house and all that he has, on every side? You have blessed the work of his hands, and his possessions have increased in the land." Then the challenge. "But put forth Your hand now and touch all that he has; he will surely curse You to Your face" (Job 1:10–11 NASB). Satan's accusation is this: God buys His worship. So Satan challenges God to remove His blessings to prove Job isn't really righteous, but merely a paid worshiper. Satan essentially says, "You have blessed Job, so he blesses You. Pull back Your blessings and Job will pull back his worship."

So God allows Satan to afflict Job with intense emotional suffering at the loss of the blessings of family and wealth. We then see Job's response in verses 20 and 21. Job tears his robe, which was an outward picture of his heart being torn. He also shaves his head, which was a sign of humility and surrender, as a man's hair was seen as his glory. Job then fell to the ground and worshiped God, saying, "Blessed be the name of the LORD" (Job 1:21 NASB). Job continues to bless God, not only when God stops blessing him but also when God takes back His blessings from him.

On another occasion, when the angels came to present themselves once again before God, Satan returns and God points out Job. This time, God doesn't merely point out his uprightness but to the fact that Job did not lose his integrity while suffering "without cause" (Job 2:3 NASB). Satan then accuses God again of buying His worship. Satan pretty much tells God, "Put Job on his deathbed, without cause, then he will curse You to Your face."

God then tells Satan, "Behold, he is in your power, only spare his life" (Job 2:6 NASB). Satan turns to afflict Job, again *without cause*, with intense physical suffering.

In both instances, Satan predicts Job will cease blessing God and curse Him to His face. Satan thinks he can humiliate God by demonstrating that mankind, the pinnacle of His creation and highest object of His love, really does not love Him in return. Unrequited love humiliates us all and Satan plans to humiliate God by demonstrating that not even God's greatest servant, Job, loves God loyally as God loves him. Satan plans to prove to God that Job only loves Him to procure material blessings.

An interesting fact here in Job is that in Hebrew the word for "curse" is *barakh*. Barakh is also the same word for "bless." Job didn't *curse* God while he suffered without cause; on the contrary, he *blessed* God without cause. No family from God. No wealth from God. No health from God. No material cause for worshiping God. No cause for blessing God, except for God being God.

When our suffering feels undeserved—when it feels without cause—we are to worship without cause. We don't worship God in order to get the cosmic kick-backs. We worship God because He is God. I know your suffering feels undeserved and royally unfair. I know trying to figure out why this is happing or what you could possibly have done to warrant this wrath is baffling. It is so hard to wrap our minds around why, if God is good, we feel so hurt by Him. Why does our happiness run from us? I know how you feel more than you realize. I've felt it my whole life—every day of my life. Often it feels so pointless. No reason for it. We don't deserve it. And because we feel we don't deserve it, it becomes so easy to want to run from

God; to want to rebel. This, however, would be the worst thing we could do. The best thing we can do is also the hardest; the thing we feel we can't do, which is to worship God even when we feel so hurt by Him.

When we feel this way it is extremely hard to convince ourselves to turn around and worship God in light of all the hurt. We have to reframe our thinking and remember that our worship isn't because God exists to provide us our happiness. If this were the case our worship would be worthless and fickle. We recognize our hurt feels like it is without cause, but remember, nevertheless, we worship without cause. This is not only what we were created to do, but also who we are created to be—God worshipers. We surrender our lives in worship not only when all is well but much more when all is not well. We worship without cause.

We are made to worship Him regardless of our circumstances and regardless of not being able to see the big picture. "Job never sees the big picture, he sees only God. But that's what we really need—for all eternity."[27] The greatest lesson for us is not to learn *why* we suffer but in suffering learn to see God—to come to know Him more deeply. We see God when we look back to all the blessings we have without cause because of Him. When we see Him and all His grace, then it only makes sense to keep on trusting and enduring; to keep on hoping and believing, to keep on worshiping. Deep down this is all we really want in our suffering: to see Him, to know Him, and to know He sees us. We can't have this without worship. We want to experience His comfort and hope when everything else hurts, but this is only realized in knowing Him deeply. We want His comfort and hope, and these are found in knowing Him and His grace. "My grace is sufficient for you, for power is perfected in weakness" (2 Corinthians 12:9 NASB).

At the end of the book of Job, God shows up in a violent whirlwind, revealing not only His power to Job, but Himself. Job then retracts his questioning as to *why* God would allow him to suffer without cause because Job now knows God more deeply. "I have heard of You by the hearing of the ear; but now my eye sees You" (Job 42:5 NASB). We see God and experience Him supernaturally in our suffering when, like Job, we bless God and do not blame Him. With a torn and humble heart, with a surrendered heart, we worship Him without cause.

NO "ZAP" FROM GOD

The other day I met an old friend at the newest, trendiest coffee house in our town. As we made our way to the back, the elongated room was rich with the fragrance of roasted coffee beans and warm lattes. Exposed, the historic brick walls seemed to absorb the industrial lighting which fastened securely upward to the stained beams crossing overhead.

As I balanced myself at a high table across from my friend, he asks if I believed God could "zap" and heal people on the spot of deep, strong, sinful desires. Or would that be God interfering with our free will? My answer to him was that of course, God could "zap" and heal anyone He chooses, and in no way would it interfere with our freedom as believers. Technically, we don't have freedom. He owns us. He bought us. The little freedom we do have is usually exercised in rebellion.

God's will for us is our sanctification. Or to put it another way, God's will for us is that we are set apart, holy like Jesus. He desires for us to look like Jesus above all else. The freedom we possess is to be used to fall in line with His plan for us by living obediently. When we sin, we look nothing like Jesus. So yeah, I believe if God wanted to expedite His will in the life of one of His own, He can do that.

I've heard of people who struggled with things like alcohol and pornography for whom one day it just clicked and they never picked up a drink or visited a pornographic website again. However, we don't see this as God's normal method of sanctification. What we see is God deepening our faith—maturing our faith—by allowing us to struggle and wrestle through the suffering of our sin. He does this with our physical suffering as well. He does this, so that when we come out on the other side, the roots of our faith will have grown deeper and stronger. As we have already seen, James 1 tells us that when trials strike, we are to endure. The word James uses for *endure* means "to remain under." Our main objective in suffering is not to look for the quickest fix or the fastest exit out from under our suffering, but to remain under it, leaning on God. Trusting in God. Hanging on to His truths. Clinging to His goodness.

James tells us when we do this, the results are not more faith but a maturing faith. We become mature believers as we endure our suffering. So can God "zap" a believer and heal him or her of their struggle with sin? Yes. Can God "zap" the suffering away in your life? Yes. Will God do that for you or your loved one? I don't know. I prayed for Him to do so countless times for Heidi and me, but He never did. And I'm thankful.

I am very thankful that there has been no "zap" from God, not only for Heidi but for me as well. If God would have "zapped" Heidi and healed her from her BPD early on, He would have circumvented the process of her maturing spiritually. Heidi's faith would have been no stronger. My faith would have been no stronger. Heidi would just be free from the unmanageability of her overwhelming emotions. God doesn't want Heidi to *just* be free from a personality disorder. He doesn't want your loved one to *just* be free from alcohol. He doesn't want a person to *just* be free from cancer. He doesn't want a person to *just* be free from depression. He wants us all to be like Jesus, because in the end being like Jesus is being free.

God doesn't share suffering just to lead us right back around to where we first started. Suffering isn't as pointless as a merry-go-round, it's not a carousel of a careless God. At least merry-go-rounds are fun. God shares suffering with us to lead us into an unforeseen joy that is only found in the freedom that comes from becoming more like Jesus. God shares suffering with us to teach us how to truly live. It acts as a catapult to launch us into a new spiritual plane of maturity. Suffering leads us to realize our need for surrendered worship, which then results in us looking more like Jesus. This means your suffering is spiritually advantageous to you. Without suffering many of us would have disastrously not advanced past the mere activity of worship to realize our true identity as God worshipers, and the freedom found therein. Suffering can take the dearest things from us, but it cannot take our worship and that is truly liberating.

The process of becoming more like Jesus begins the same way you became a Christian: faith. "Therefore as you have received Christ Jesus the Lord, *so* walk in Him" (Colossians 2:6 NASB). Faith is what saved us, and faith is what carries us through the process of maturing spiritually into being like Jesus. It is a lifelong process, which in the end will be completed by

God Himself. As I said, faith carries us through the process, and at the heart of the process is learning to surrender in worship. It is responding to God with our life. God is not a facet of our life; He is not an attachment or an appendage for Sundays, He is our life. Worship is the surrender of our former life with its dreams, things *supposed to* be, and selfish desires. We leave behind the things suffering threatens or has taken, to follow Jesus. We surrender our life to Him, not because He gives us cause by promising cosmic kick-backs, but because He is God and we are not. We surrender in worship because of who He is, not because we look to profit from a transactional "blessings for worship" relationship.

Pride is our biggest obstacle to living a lifestyle of surrender. Pride is cunning and we are often in denial of it. Pride tricks us into thinking it isn't there. We all have pride. Somehow, during Heidi's first night in that decrepit and dilapidated treatment facility, between the man walking in on her in her own bathroom and the guy vomiting all night outside her bedroom, God broke a major part of her pride. When she was about to choke down a fist full of quarters and end it all, by the grace of God, she threw down the quarters, threw up her hands, and said, "I give up."

Suffering can destroy your dream life but it can't destroy your worship. Satan can steal your loved one away, but he can't steal from you your worship. Suffering can empty your bank account and you of your energy, but it can't empty you of your worship. So you worship. I'm talking about worshiping Him in the midst of your pain and hurt, with an unwavering commitment to praising and thanking Him for the goodness and love He has for you without cause. I'm talking about responding to God with all you have when you have nothing left to offer but your life.

He truly has your worship when He has your life, and when He has your life, you find His.

Suffering has altered your life because sin produces death in everything good and brings about rot where life should flourish. Jesus has come to alter you back into His image—back to life. It happens when we surrender in worshiping without cause in response to who God is; a God who loves without cause.

We surrender in worship to God because we are created to worship without cause. The beauty is that now, through Jesus, we find even more reason to worship Him for who He is. God has chosen to bless us with every spiritual blessing in the heavenly places without cause (Ephesians 1:3 NASB). How much more, then, should we surrender in worship, not just because He is God, but because He is a good God so rich in grace? Through Jesus, God has chosen to demonstrate His immense love, a love without cause. He loves us, not because of anything we have done or will ever do; our worship is not even a cause for His love. He loves us purely because of His goodness and the richness of His grace. This is who He is, He is love. This is why we worship Him. He is a good God whose character never changes, whose grace never disparages, and whose love never diminishes, even when we feel we are least deserving.

I know your suffering feels like it is without cause, a carousel from a careless God, but it is not. There is a reason for all of this, you are becoming more like Jesus, the one who suffered without cause to demonstrate God's supreme love for you which is without cause. So don't curse God because your suffering is without cause; bless God because He is a good God rich in grace and He loves you immensely—without cause.

CHAPTER 10

We Count Days

THIS LAST SUMMER, HEIDI, ALONG WITH HER SISTERS AND DAD, climbed a fourteener in honor of her grandfather, who passed away a year earlier. Her grandfather climbed countless mountains whose heights exceeded 14,000 feet, hence the name fourteener and why they climbed one. I believe there are fifty-eight fourteeners in Colorado, and Quandary Peak is one of those. There was some apprehension as to whether or not Heidi should make the trek. Her neutrophil count (a subset of white blood cells) had been extremely low in prior months due to her consumption of hand sanitizer. Heidi had not touched the junk for some time by the climb but got evaluated by a doctor just in case. Her blood levels looked good, so she joined the climb.

Climbing fourteeners is still daunting even for people in good health. Not only is there the threat of dying from being struck by lightning if you don't get off the mountain by the time the afternoon storm rolls in, but there is also altitude sickness. The worst-case scenario with altitude sickness is your lungs fill with fluid and you die. Aside from the physical threats of climbing a fourteener, there are psychological effects that can hinder a person from reaching the summit.

The group got an extra early start that morning to make sure they gave themselves enough time to reach the summit. They lost a little bit of time because they got lost in the dark and couldn't find the trail, but once on the trail, they began their ascent up Quandary. At this stage, they were in the trees and visibility was limited. No one could see the summit, but obviously, they knew it was there. After climbing above the tree line, the terrain became rocky and unstable. Every step had to be taken with focus as the rocks underfoot would move and shift. The unstable footing, the shaky knees, the burning legs, and difficulty breathing after a while slowed their progress. At some points, they would count ten steps then take a break. They would then count ten more steps, stop, and breathe. The counting steps helped in order to set a pace. Climbing 14,265 feet ten steps at a time can be trying. Seeing the summit, however, reenergized Heidi. That is until her sister informed her it was a false summit.

The peak Heidi climbed was appropriately named Quandary. A quandary is a state of uncertainty in a difficult situation. Not only was Quandary filled with uncertainty while enduring the difficult climb, especially the higher Heidi got, Quandary was also a metaphor for the last few years of our life together. Starting out lost in the dark, moving unable to see the goal, eventually rising above the trees and able to see for the first time in a long time, but still struggling, still slipping and stumbling. We've felt the hope that comes in seeing the goal, the finish line ahead of us. And we've felt the disappointment at the discovery it was yet another false summit.

There is a really cool picture of Heidi walking on the top

of the mountain overlooking a breathtaking scene below. I love the picture because she's treading the heights but hasn't reached the top yet. She's still in the process of climbing, but the beauty found by her in the midst of her struggle to the top is captured in the moment. Our spiritual transformation or alteration is the beauty in the suffering. The goal of looking more like Jesus is what makes it worth it, it's what keeps us going; it is what keeps us continuing the climb as we gain little tastes of His joy and the potential of more. It is what gives us light while trying to navigate the dark confusion and struggle of it all.

Life is a quandary. It is full of difficulties and uncertainties. We don't always know how to handle situations and navigate through tough stretches and climbs. We count each step, pacing ourselves when climbing through our quandaries. When Heidi lost her footing on some rocks, she didn't say, "I lost my step and have to start over." She kept going. When we slip we don't turn around either and start the climb all over. That wouldn't make sense. We keep climbing and clawing; we keep digging in and pushing through the headaches and nausea. Shaky knees and trouble breathing aren't signs we are not climbing well enough and need to start over. They are signs we're not backing down in the face of adversity. We don't turn back because the climb doesn't look perfect or we didn't do it in stellar health or record time; we fight until we reach the summit.

When we reach false summits and our hopes turn to disappointments, we don't start over and try again, hoping to make the climb with a better attitude. When we slip along our way up, we keep pushing forward, focused on the goal while enjoying the beauty of how far God has brought us. We hope in reaching the summit but have joy in the climb. Even when we lose our footing and flat out fall, we don't "start over." We don't go back to the base of the mountain and try again. I know at times it feels like we do, but we don't. When we fall, we get up and count our steps. We even count the bad steps or the missteps so we learn not to fall again. The psalmist wrote, "If I should say, 'My foot has slipped,' Your lovingkindness, O LORD, will hold me up" (Psalm 94:18 NASB). When we slip and fall along the way, we know the one whose loyal love holds us.

THE FALL

Ninety-five days before Heidi's climb was day 51 of being clean. We had counted fifty-one days. Heidi was rolling in her recovery. Staying clean wasn't easy, but it was happening in a way that had never happened before. This was the most momentum she had established ever. Thursday, day 50, Heidi woke up not feeling well. She worked all day long. Heidi still worked for the company she started out as a temp almost ten years before when we moved to Dallas. She worked from her home office they set up for her. This particular day she was in her office from before sun up until 9:00 that night. I don't know what was so important, but I know she sat at her desk for hours. She also had been running a temperature of one hundred degrees most of the day. That night she turned out the office light, closed the double doors behind her, walked into the bedroom, and crashed on the bed.

Early Friday morning, day 51, I awakened as Heidi got out of bed. Half-awake, I hear her quietly pass by the foot of our bed on her way into the bathroom adjacent to my side of the bed. I doze back off briefly then awaken once again to the sound of the battery-powered thermometer beeping. I hear it beep a couple of times then I hear her body drop. Hard. If you can picture a sniper taking a person out with a headshot in a movie and the body falling limp, dropping to the ground without caution, that's what it sounded like. I immediately jump out of bed, dart the ten feet into the bathroom, and flip on the light. As the light flashes on I see at my feet Heidi on her back convulsing violently.

"Heidi! Heidi! Heidi!" I'm yelling at her, but she's not responding. Her eyes fixed straight forward up at the ceiling; her arms are rigid and hands gnarled, slowly curling up to her face. Her body is shaking uncontrollably as she gasps and gurgles for air. I grab her right arm by the wrist to try and keep it from curling up to her face as if that will magically reverse whatever is going on. Her eyes begin to roll to the back of her head as she gives up trying to breathe. "Heidi! Can you hear me? If you can hear me, just relax and focus on breathing." I'm flooded by a million terrifying thoughts, *Is she dying? What will I tell my son? What will I say to the twins on their wedding days?*

These million thoughts raced through my head in a rush. Then I thought, *Is she having a seizure?* I've heard of people throwing up and choking to death on their own vomit during seizures. Not sure if it's true, I begin to gently roll her over on her left side. As her shoulders lift up followed by her head, I see blood. I also see it on the tile where her head hit. I lay her gently back. I run to grab a towel. Her eyes are lifeless as her bleeding worsens. I fold the towel into a thick small square and place it under her head like a pillow. She's still not responding, still convulsing, and her eyes are still trying to roll back. After I frantically, yet gently, situate the folded towel under her head, I rush out of the bathroom to grab my phone from my bedside and call 911.

Heidi's eyes are now becoming unfixed. Her breathing is shallow and labored as her eyes, lost, look over toward me. I'm pretending to be calm to keep her calm. She still can't talk or answer me. When she tries, the only sound she can make is a gurgling gasp. She's now lying perfectly still. The look on her face is a mixture of both confusion and terror. She looks lost. When the 911 dispatcher tells me the responders are close, I tell Heidi not to move while I run to the front door. I open the door so they don't lose time entering. I shove the couch out of the way like some linebacker on my way back to Heidi in the master bath.

When I return to Heidi, so does her speech. She asks what had happened. I tell her she fell and hit her head, but she will be fine. "Okay," she says. A few moments later, with her head perfectly still, her eyes move up to their right corners to look at me; she asks again what had happened. Once again, I tell her she fell and hit her head but will be fine. She responds, "Okay," once more. A few moments go by and she asks, "What happened?" After the EMT evaluates her, the only thing she knows is my first name and hers. That's it. No date. No president's name. No mom's name. She only knows her first name and mine.

With the way she was lying and the door's position, they could not get the stretcher in the bathroom. The EMTs stabilize her neck in a brace then wrap her in a sheet to lift her off the ground. They lift her and carry her into the master bedroom to place her on the stretcher.

We arrive at the emergency department around 6:30 a.m. Her memory slowly returned to her over the course of the morning. Upon being discharged from the ED, the doctor told me to watch her closely because her major concussion would certainly affect her behavior. The next morning she scored some hand sanitizer.

She broke her longest streak of counting days outside of her pregnancies. Back to day 1. I hate counting days. She had to start her counting over. The ensuing shame and self-hate aggrandized by her then undiagnosed BPD was all too unbearable. Heidi sat on our living room floor, dejected and head hung low; a chorus of shrill cries came out between her labored grasps for breath. The tears coursed over and down her cheeks to her chin where she neither bothered to erase nor acknowledge them as they fell, one by one, into her lap.

THE RESOLUTION CHAPTER

After a shaky start, Heidi started over. She conquered Quandary eighty-seven days later and kept on cruising. She was doing so well I waited to write this chapter. This was *supposed to* be the last chapter I write. The rest is finished. I was waiting to write this chapter because this would be the resolution chapter. I was going to tell the story of this big party with all these people packed in our house celebrating 365 consecutive good days of no mess ups. I was going to brag about 365 consecutive miracles.

The scene in this chapter would be set with me standing on a chair as I ask for everyone's attention. Once everyone quiets down and looks toward me I then go into a short, but great speech, that both brags on Heidi as well as thanks everyone for their support. I would thank those people who were hands-on with Heidi over the past year, the people who made it a priority to get coffee with Heidi, and those who exercised with Heidi. I would also thank others for being not so much hands-on but more on their faces praying for Heidi and for God to work a miracle in her life. This was the chapter that was going to be written on Heidi's one-year sobriety birthday.

That's what I was going to say on that day, but on that date, there will be no celebration. There will be no packed house and no speech. Today, after a very long streak of good days, Heidi lost her date. These bad days are why I hate counting days. When you start recovery, counting days is so hard because you feel like it is so impossible to get traction, which then leads to you feeling and thinking like it is not even worth the struggle, not worth the climb. But you do it anyway. Then after a significant amount of days, if lost, it feels like a punishment or a mark of shame having to say you must start over. For a person plagued by intensified shame and preyed upon by BPD, counting days is too much. The internalization of it is too overwhelming. It's too much to say, "I lost my date and I have to start over."

So, no. Not anymore. We're not starting over. We're going to keep moving forward. We are not counting days; I hate counting days. We are going to, instead, make the days count. We believe God is in control and He makes bad days count for good, just as much as He makes the good days count. So we believe there can be no day so bad that it derails God's plan to alter our lives into lives that look like His Son's. God is making all days count, good and bad. So we not only count good days; we count all days because we believe God is making them all count for our good.

We make all days count by entrusting them to God. We make them count when we choose to follow Jesus, not just into the good days but even when He is leading us into those dark days we just don't want to follow. Those bad days that make us feel like hope and healing are just illusions and a mirage. Those bad days that make it so hard to hope. But these bad days we feel like we can no longer get our hopes up are, in fact, the days that God uses to catapult us to a new spiritual plane of maturity. But we have to keep going; we have to keep trusting and climbing. He's using these days to radically alter you through your suffering. We believe that, like the ostrich, these bad days that appear so out of control and reckless are not apart from God's sovereign plan. We believe not even the bad days can rob us of this truth: that our God is with us, fights for us, and He has a good plan for us.

And so, on the days when we can't see God working or feel Him comforting, we still worship Him because we know these bad days ultimately count for our good because He is good. We surrender our desires and dreams for this life over to a God whose end game is making us look like Jesus. And the unforeseen joy that will result is far better than what we can imagine or have planned for ourselves. Jesus came not that we might just have life but that we would have it abundantly, experiencing the supernatural joy of His life living in us. We worship without cause because we exist for a God who is rich in immeasurable grace and immense love for us without cause. We do not worship Him because we falsely assume Him to be the harbinger of our happiness. We worship without cause because He is God and we have been created to exist at this moment in history to bring about His fame, not our own.

Heidi may have lost her date, but she has not lost all God has done in her life. She hasn't lost all the transformation that has preceded this point. She may have lost her date, but we have seen miracles. We've seen a life marked by "disorder" gradually regain order. With that order we see a new person emerge who loves those hard to love because she knows she's been hard to love. When she can, Heidi meets the pressing needs of others, whether answering the call to give a ride to another mom who is in a tough spot or cook and deliver a meal to a family in a pinch. She does so because she knows the love she's felt when others stepped in during the lowly moments of her own journey. She prays that God would work miracles in her life and in the lives of those around her. She is a better mom and wife before all this began. She's more like Jesus than she was before this all began.

A major step taken along her journey has been learning to love herself. Self-love frees Heidi to forgive herself, rather than cosign herself to the insurmountable task of absolving herself of her own failings. Self-destruction and self-punishment or any self-punitive action is not an option for those who know they are loved. She is learning that believing what God says about her is infinitely more valuable than what others are saying. Heidi can finally drop the mask of misdirection. She can let loose the insidious haunt of always having to be more, either as an employee, a mom, or just a person. She works hard to live by grace, shutting down perfectionism's daily whispers of inadequacy and reducing to rubble shame's accusations of past shortcomings. Heidi is becoming stronger than ever. She is becoming a fighter more than ever.

So I don't care if she has lost her date or has to "start over" because she's started over before, and it has led her to become the most amazing and courageous woman I know. Yes, there are mess ups. Yes, there will be mess ups. Yes, Heidi will keep learning and growing from those mess ups. Eventually, there will come about a new normal without mess ups. That's just the nature and process of our suffering. And most likely it is the same with yours. Your bad days and mess ups are advantageous for your growth and transformation. You can't let a bad day count against you, you turn it around and make it count for you because that's what God wants to do.

To quote Heidi's favorite song from Life.Church Worship, "The battle rages but You have won the war." Our battle rages on—and may very well rage for the rest of our lives—but we believe our God has won the war. It's one thing to sing it, but a totally radical thing to believe it and with eyes full of tears thank God for it. This is why we can hope even when it feels impossible to get our hopes up because the love of God has been poured out within our hearts (Romans 5:5).

Heidi never drinking or consuming hand sanitizer again to relieve the range of inescapable volatile emotions is not the resolution to our story. The resolution to our story is not some miracle fairy-tale book ending either. The resolution to our story is that by the grace of God—through our suffering—Heidi and I are being radically altered into the image of Jesus.

Your summit is the same. God wants, above all, for you to look and love like Jesus looks and loves. God is not afraid to use something as drastic as cancer, death, disease, infertility, a personality disorder, a congenital disorder—or whatever else we may fear—to make this happen. Where suffering drastically alters your life, God's grace stands ready to radically alter you.

HOLD YOU ME

It is comforting to know that God makes the bad days count just as much as the good ones. It is reassuring that a bad day to us could be that pivotal moment or event that God uses to change everything for our good. It helps to know that we have a God who is working all things together for our good—for our transformation. However, it still doesn't take the edge off some of those just really atrocious days. Those days the anxiety is so gut-wrenching and thought robbing. The days you feel so hopeless you can't get yourself to get out of bed. The days the physical pain is just unpalatable. So what do we do in the meantime? What do we do when we find ourselves in those just really hard days; the days before we see the good we so desperately want to see God work? During these tough days, we say to God, "Hold You me."

My son, when he was younger and beginning to put words together, would come to me when something bad happened. Maybe he pinched his finger and it hurt. Maybe he fell and scraped a knee. Maybe he lost a toy car. When something bad happened, he would stand right in front of me, look up at me, arms reaching up toward me, and say, "Daddy, hold you me." He obviously was trying to say, "Hold me," but had heard me say, "Hold you?" for so long he put it all together into, "Hold you me."

If you have little ones or have had them, chances are they have said the same thing to you. My two little girls are at the stage where they are saying it now. As a dad, I love it. I love to pick my children up and kiss the scrape or the mystery wound they are pointing to. You pick them up and carry them for as long as it takes to comfort them and see them through the pain. When we are in the middle of our bad days, there are really not a lot of healthy ways to take the edge off, but we can always go to our heavenly daddy and ask Him to *hold You me.*

By the time you get to chapter 46 in the book of Isaiah, God has already told His people that He will be using the empire of Babylon to judge them for abandoning Him to worship other gods. He then tells His people that He will eventually judge Babylon with another world superpower for how they will mistreat Israel. Isaiah 46 is that scene. God mocks Babylon's gods, Bel and Nebo, who will have to be carried on the backs of cattle to flee their coming invader. In verses 3 and 4, God makes the contrast of Himself to other gods by reminding His people that He has been the one who has carried them from the womb and will continue to carry them into their old age as a nation.

Others have to carry their gods, but we have a God who carries His people. You have a God who carries you. The end of verse 4 says, "I will carry you and rescue you" (Isaiah 46:4 NET). God carries His worn out people who have been displaced, hurt, and abused; His people who are weary, exhausted, and confused. As a dad who loves to carry his children when they hurt or are sad, I know God has to love carrying His children far more. God always carries us, and He promises to continue to do so, even into our old age. He will never leave us or abandon us, according to Hebrews 13:5.

Maybe you can't help but feel abandoned. Perhaps your bad days are a result of your bad choices. Maybe you have done some bad things for a while now that you know have been wrong. You're wondering how God can still love you. Perhaps you've been messing up for some time and feel God has given up on you. God doesn't give up, and He won't give up on you. He carries you because He loves you.

The Hebrew word for *carry* in Isaiah 46 has the idea of carrying a load or something that you and I might say is too burdensome to carry. Not for God. Whatever burden you believe you are to God, you are not too heavy for Him to carry. Whatever burden you are attempting to carry on your own, it is not too heavy to let God carry for you. Your bad days might be a result of your bad choices, but you are not your choices. You are loved. Your bad days, your circumstances, are not a reflection of God's love for you either. If your circumstances reflected God's love for you, then His love would, without warning, ebb and flow; drift and drag with your circumstances.

The cross is the reflection of God's love for you. The love that moved God to make a sacrifice of His Son on your behalf at the cross never changes. We don't look at our circumstances; we look to the cross to see the measure of God's love. There we see the full measure—the full demonstration—of God's love for us in that while we were still sinners, Christ died for us (Romans 5:8).

Today is a day, personally, when I keep asking God to carry me. Carry my wife. Carry my family. Carry my marriage. It's not that I think He isn't carrying me or I'm asking so that He will; I ask because it acts as a reminder and comfort to myself. Some days I have to remind myself that my God carries me. Many days I need the comfort that He's always there carrying me. On these days, I simply say, "God, carry me. Hold You me," and it reminds and comforts me that He's never stopped. He's still going; He's still carrying.

So I don't know what kind of day you're having or what kind of days or weeks you've been having, but you have a heavenly daddy you can go stand directly in front of, look up to, arms reaching high, and say, "Hold You me." Hopefully, you will receive the same comfort that I do from this truth, that we have a God who carries His weary children. I hope knowing your God is carrying you, right this moment, takes some of the edge off while He continues to work to make these bad days count.

CHAPTER 11

Ruler over the Realm

GOING BACK TO THAT NEFARIOUS DATE OF NOVEMBER 8, HEIDI and I sat in church just days after. We know how bad the situation has escalated. The staff and the elders both know how bad the situation has escalated. That Sunday morning, the passage being taught was Daniel 4. If you are not familiar with Daniel 4, basically the king of Babylon, Nebuchadnezzar, loses his mind, and after seven years God restores his reason. What makes this a special story is that God gave Nebuchadnezzar a dream twelve months prior, and through Daniel, God tells Nebuchadnezzar he would lose his mind if he didn't stop his evil. Nebuchadnezzar refuses to change his mind so God takes his mind, giving it back seven years later. When Nebuchadnezzar's mind is restored to him, he then directs everyone to praise Daniel's God, declaring Him the Most High.

There are a number of reasons, and many unknown, why God allows suffering, but a big reason we do know is this: God uses our suffering to radically alter us so that through our stories we will direct people's praise toward God, the Most High. He uses your story so that everyone may know He is the ruler over the realm of mankind (Daniel 4:17 NASB).

The lights in church auditorium flickered from dim to bright. The room is quiet with a distant cough and occasional faint throat clearing. A few seats down a mother whispers something softly to her child. The air smells of coffee and upholstered chairs. You can hear the seats adjusting and creaking as church members settle in while the pastor climbs the four or five steps to the stage. As the sermon played out, I remember sitting next to Heidi, quietly listening in the back left of the auditorium, thinking, *It has been about seven years now. I wish God would restore my wife.*

Nebuchadnezzar was being celebrated for losing his mind and acting crazy because it demonstrated that our God was the Most High and indeed the ruler over the realm of mankind. But from where we sat, the same God who is ruler over the realm in Daniel 4 was not in our realm. No one came up to us and said, "I know this is a crazy difficult time, but it will be okay. Our God is ruler over the realm. He is powerful enough to restore you and your family. He can rebuild the ruins."

It felt as if people were talking more about us than what big thing God might be about to do through us. And so, it didn't feel like God was using our suffering to bring attention to Himself. It felt like the opposite. It felt like all eyes were on us, not God. It all seemed so pointless. Most days it seemed impossible. It may feel the same for you right now. Pointless. Impossible. All eyes on you and not what God is about to do through you. God uses the pointless and impossible. A lot. So you might just be right where you want if you want to be more like Jesus.

In Daniel 4, how pointless was it that the king through whom God plans to direct people's attention to Himself is hidden away, where I'm sure no one could see him? I mean the king thought he was an animal and was eating the grass throughout the palace grounds like a cow. That wouldn't exactly reflect well on the empire if people knew. The king's hair is like eagle feathers, and his nails are grotesquely long. They are described as looking like bird claws. This hairy, "taloned," king who is constantly drenched in the dew of the earth, is a textbook definition of a lost cause. His situation looks impossible. Even though God said it would only last seven years, if we would have been there, we likely would have been wondering how it all was going to bring God glory. How will God raise this man up from the dewy ruins and seat him once again as king on the iron throne from which he had fallen so far? It seemed more likely the king would make a better groundskeeper in the kingdom since he's good at keeping the grass low. Then, when it seemed so pointless and impossible, Nebuchadnezzar writes, "But at the end of that period, I, Nebuchadnezzar, raised my eyes toward heaven and my reason returned to me, and I blessed the Most High and praised and honored Him who lives forever" (Daniel 4:34 NASB).

At times I wished God would just zap us. I wish He would zap all our sin and suffering away. (Then we could tell everyone how Jesus zapped us. As if people don't think Christians are odd enough, we go around telling people Jesus zapped us.) I think He still can and still does do this. I know one day when He returns He will do it once for all. Until that day I just don't see this being His typical way of dealing with our suffering.

God draws our attention and the attention of those around us to the impossibility of diseases, hardships, and troubled relationships; and He allows that suffering to continue so the bystanders can see the impossibility of it all. God works like this so that at just the right time—through our faithful endurance—all that attention, all those eyes fixed on our suffering, will pivot to His power living in us. Attention is given to His deliverance, perhaps not *from* suffering but His deliverance *in* the midst of our suffering. The deliverance of His grace to keep us going; to sustain us. Suffering is missional to God. So when we who have suffered, along with Nebuchadnezzar, say that we will bless God the Most High (regardless of how our circumstances are playing out) and worship without cause Him who lives forever, those around us will know exactly why our God is indeed the ruler over the realm of mankind.

SAVE THE SNOW

All everyone had been talking about was the snow.

"Are you ready for the snow?"
"I heard the snow will be moving in this afternoon."
"I heard the snow will start falling tonight."

You do not have to live in Oklahoma long before you learn not to get your hopes up on the snow forecast. It is just easier to not get your hopes up and be pleasantly surprised than to get excited and wake up to nothing. Nothing is usually what happens after the hyped forecast of snow. So naturally, I was a bit trepid. We hadn't seen snow in our part of Oklahoma in four years. Before that, I have no idea how many years it had been.

I woke up a little before 6:00 that morning. As I walked out of the bedroom and into the kitchen to make coffee before reading, to my surprise, I saw the snow falling out of our kitchen door window. Lit only by the orange halo of the streetlights, the snow fell strong and with grace. I moved to Heidi's office, shutting the double doors behind me. I sat at the desk, distracted by the snow's relentlessness out the window. The snow was quickly accumulating on the ground, the trees, and grew wildly on the street sign. It was entrancing how the snow quickly and fiercely appeared out of the darkness into the orange hue of our streetlight only for a fleeting moment before finding its final resting place among the already settled snow.

An hour later I walked out of the office to be met by my son as he, half-awake, staggered around the hall corner. I caught his sleepy, squinty eyes as he saw the heavy snow that fell magnificently. He couldn't remember the snow that fell four years earlier. He was so excited, but he'd have to wait until after school to play in the snow.

The snow darted mesmerizingly at our windshield like an old Windows 98 screen saver. The drive to school that morning was as silent as the serene scene before us. The heavy, deep grey sky hung low with no regard for the sun. The whole landscape sat paralyzed before us, having yielded its strength to the might of the snow which held it down. The snow seemed to majestically hit pause on the whole world around us, holding it in a dream-like stillness. Its beauty's pausing effect was not even lost on the stilled five-year-old in the backseat. It was like we had stumbled through a wardrobe of our own into a magical new world.

The snow tapered off by noon but kept all day. That night while we put our son to bed, he realized he hadn't made a snowman. How he didn't think to build a snowman I don't know.

Heidi promised him tomorrow he and his dad would build a snowman. We prayed and he fell asleep.

The next morning after I dropped him off at school, I realized on the drive home that the snow was melting quickly. At the rate of its melting, there wouldn't be enough left to build a snowman that afternoon. Once home I got out of my car, grabbed the snow shovel, walked through the house to the backyard, and started scooping snow. I carried scoop after scoop to the north side of the house where the sun's warm reach couldn't touch it. I kept telling myself that I had enough, but I still kept going back to shovel more snow. It dawned on me I was no longer trying to save a little snow to build a snowman, I was trying to save all the snow. I was trying to save all the snow because it was so beautiful and rarely do we get the chance to enjoy it in Oklahoma.

It looked so pure and refreshing, so innocent the way it just sat there hiding the dead grass. It softly piled up with ease as the shovel glided effortlessly underneath. I knew I was being stupid and that the snow would eventually melt even if I hid it in a place the sun couldn't find it. I caught a thought on one of my trips back to my hoard of snow. *Beautiful things are worth saving, even if it feels like a lost cause.*

A few days after my vain attempt to save the snow, and long after the snow had melted, I told this story to a friend of mine after lunch. We pulled out of the parking lot for me to drop him back off at work. As we rolled out of the lot I told him how Heidi is beautiful to me and I may have a problem because I keep fighting for her when at times her personality disorder seemed so dominating, so impossible; so much like a lost cause.

"I can't stop shoveling the snow," I tell him.

"I can't stop saving the snow. I can't stop trying to save Heidi even though it all feels like a lost cause most days. I know I can't save her, but I can't stop trying."

After a pause, he softly said, "I think you are worth saving."

Maybe you have a loved one who feels like a lost cause. Perhaps you yourself feel like a lost cause. Perhaps you are facing or up against something impossible, maybe something seemingly pointless. Maybe what you've been called to suffer will never be "fixed." Regardless, *you* are worth saving. Your spiritual growth and transformation are worth the fight. Your impossible situation may feel like a lost cause. You may feel like a lost cause. Your loved one may feel like a lost cause. You may feel God has given up on you because your suffering continues and your prayers have gone unanswered. You may feel like you are a lost cause because you feel, either God doesn't seem to hear you or you don't deserve to be heard. You, however, are worth saving. God believes you are worth delivering. Don't give up. God's children are not lost causes. It's not knowing *why* we suffer that we must seek, but knowing *how* we must suffer and *who* strengthens us to do so. It is through *how* well we suffer that the Holy Spirit can bring everyone's attention to the truth of *who* our God is and that He is indeed the ruler over the realm of mankind.

You are not a lost cause. He will rescue you. Somehow, God keeping you right where you are, although it hurts, is the best thing for you to become more like His Son and to experience the life He has for you. And in doing so, others can see the life He has waiting for them too. Until this is over for you, remember He carries you. When you are overburdened, He carries you. When you are weighed down, He carries you. The heavier life becomes for you, the tighter He holds on to you.

There is no hurt He can't heal and no disease He can't defeat. There is no relationship He can't restore and no sorrow He can't soothe. And even if He doesn't, there is no hurt He can't sustain us in and no disease He can't strengthen us to endure. There is no broken relationship He can't empower us to love in and no sorrow He can't soothe us with joy.

There are many days my suffering has me weighed down. Some days, all I can do is just watch my wife suffer, and feel powerless to help. On those days, I remind myself of the one who always carries me, and I repeat to myself a couple of verses that have helped me steer my thoughts away from resentment and envy or just wanting to give up altogether. Here is a go-to for me: "But as for me, I will watch expectantly for the LORD; I will wait for the God of my salvation. My God will hear me. Do not rejoice over me, O my enemy. Though I fall I will rise; though I dwell in darkness, the LORD is a light for me" (Micah 7:7–8 NASB). I will rise and as I wait in this dark place, I have an everlasting light that will not go out on me. That constant light is a reminder to me that at just the right moment, the darkness will be disposed and my God will raise me up; He will raise these ruins because beautiful things are worth saving. Beautiful things are worth raising. And even if He doesn't deliver me *from* my suffering, He promises to deliver me *in* my suffering.

RAISE THE RUINS

No one seemed to be more of a lost cause than the kingdom of Judah. They ignored countless second chances from God. They had the best prophets sent to tell them exactly what God desired for them. Nothing ever worked in the long run. After King Solomon, the kingdom of Israel split into two kingdoms. The southern kingdom, Judah, took its name after the tribe of Judah and consisted of only itself and Benjamin. The northern kingdom consisted of all the other tribes of Israel. The north would eventually be conquered by the Assyrian empire. The southern kingdom continued on for another hundred years before God brought a new world superpower, Babylon, to take His people into exile because of their rejection of Him to worship foreign gods.

In his book, Isaiah forewarns of the Assyrian conquest of the north and lives to see it. He also forewarns of the coming relentless Babylonian invasion and the leveling of Judah's cities. Isaiah, however, isn't just a prophet of judgment; he is also a prophet of restoration. You can easily break the gigantic book of Isaiah into two parts: judgment (chapters 1—39) and restoration (chapters 40—66).

In the restoration section of Isaiah, God comforts His people by telling them that after they go into exile, He will bring them back from Babylon and restore them to their land. There is a verse that I love, which says, "Confirming the word of His servant and performing the purpose of His messengers. *It is I* who says of Jerusalem, 'She shall be inhabited!' And of the cities of Judah, 'They shall be built.' And I will raise up her ruins *again*" (Isaiah 44:26 NASB). God says of His holy city, Jerusalem, where death and desolation are rife, "She shall be inhabited." He will raise up life again. And of these cities that are leveled and destroyed, God says, "I will raise up her ruins again." God did not abandon His people in exile, and seventy years later, He brought them back and slowly began to raise the ruins. He didn't just raise the ruins of their cities; He raised the ruins of their nation. Through leaders like Ezra, Nehemiah, Zerubbabel, and others, God raised up the ruins of His people's spirits. God is a God of restoration and rebuilding. And one day, still in the future, God will fully restore and rebuild His nation, Israel. And everyone will see it.

People can't look away from suffering. Next time you drive by a car wreck, try not looking. Like already mentioned, God uses that attention given toward suffering to turn that same attention then to Himself. He is the God who raises up the ruins. He is the God who speaks into the recesses in His people's lives where death and desolation are rife and says, "She shall be inhabited!" Of marriages that are as good as dead, "She shall be inhabited!" When cancer levels a person's body and robs them of their dignity, it is God who says, "I will raise up her ruins again." Of people who fight anxiety and depression, "I will raise up her ruins again." Where addiction has leveled a life, "I will raise up her ruins again." All this, so when people see the new thing God has done out of a person's suffering, everyone will know that He, and only He, is the ruler of the realm of mankind. God says, "Is there any God besides Me, or is there any *other* Rock? I know of none" (Isaiah 44:8 NASB).

I pray a lot of small prayers. Here is an example: "Carry my marriage. Carry my wife. Carry me, God." Another one that is consistently prayed is this: "Jesus, I believe You will raise up these ruins." A fair warning and one you might need to get ready to accept: God does not always raise up the ruins how we believe He should. That loved one suffering from cancer might not be raised up victoriously over his or her illness. They may actually succumb to the disease, but that doesn't mean God isn't raising up the ruins out of your tragedy and their story. Your unfaithful spouse may never get his or her act together, but that doesn't mean God isn't raising up the ruins in your life to do amazing things in order to draw attention and glory to Himself.

A big part of following Jesus when He's leading us where we do not want to go is saying, "I'm trusting you as the builder with the reconstruction project because you are God and I am not." We trust God with the outcome even if the outcome is not what we want at that exact moment. God will not always fix it how we would like, but if you will follow Him and trust Him, He will radically alter you into a new person whose ruins have been raised, a person who has been raised to be like Jesus.

Like for Jesus, God does not always deliver us out from under the cross He has called us to carry. God does not always promise to deliver us out from our suffering, but He does promise to always deliver us while in our suffering. His grace sustains us and empowers us to be raised up—not always out from the ruins—but always in the midst of them and always with good reason. Jesus was, literally, raised up in the midst of His suffering that He would draw all men to Himself (John 12:32). As God begins to raise you up in the midst of your suffering He will continue to draw others to Himself through you.

Another great verse out of the restoration section of Isaiah is this: "See, I am doing a new thing! Now it springs up; do you not perceive it? I am making a way in the wilderness and streams in the wasteland" (Isaiah 43:19 NIV). God was doing a new thing with His people, and it was hard for them to see it because of the present pain of exile, but He hadn't given up on them. When all Judah saw was a wilderness, God saw a way. When all Judah could perceive was their own solemn existence in a wasteland, God was making streams to sustain them. Rarely do we get the luxury of seeing what God is doing behind the scenes of our suffering. I can tell you this though: He hasn't given up on you. You are worth saving; you are worth delivering and raising up. You may not see it—you may not even feel it—but God is doing a new thing. God is radically altering you into a powerful follower of Jesus right now in the midst of your suffering. You may not see it today while in the wilderness. You may not perceive it now while you're in your own personal wasteland, but He's working. He doesn't stop working to impart life in you; to raise you up! Jesus said, "My Father is working until now, and I Myself am working" (John 5:17 NASB).

The ruler over the realm doesn't stop. He won't stop until your life directs and draws people back to Himself through His Son. People will see you, raised up again (either out from or within the ruins), and they will see Jesus. When Job tore his robe, it wasn't just an outward picture of an inward torn heart. The tearing of his robe in two was also a dramatic outward image of the suffering that tore his life in two. When we suffer, there is always a loss being suffered. There is a sense in which we are torn from something or someone; something or someone is torn from us. A child is torn from us. Our health is torn from us. A dream is torn from us. When we suffer, on top of our suffering is the suffering of life being torn in two. Suffering is the tearing apart of life as we have known it.

Since suffering first reared its ugly head, we've seen how it tears lives apart. When sin entered the world, and death through sin, we saw the relationship between God and both Adam and Eve tear in two. We saw Adam and Eve suffer a severing in their own relationship as well. Sin brings death, and with death comes its shadow, suffering. Since death and suffering first entered the world stage, there was also a promise given—the promise of a sending. A grand deliverer would be sent to reverse the curse of death. Until then, there would be enmity—a spiritual war—in the meantime. Then at just the right time, God would send. God sent His Son, Jesus. His mission: destroy the works of the devil, destroy death, and bring life (1 John 3:8).

God's mission in sending His Son involved suffering. Jesus was made a despicable spectacle in His suffering of the cross, but through it, He made a public spectacle of death. The gospel tells us that suffering plays a major front and center role in the mission of God. Our suffering, if we choose to faithfully endure it, brings glory to God and destroys death in others by making clear the message of life in us by faith. There is no greater honor than to be chosen to suffer for your Savior, who first suffered on your behalf to destroy death in you by freely giving life to you. Your suffering is another kind of sending of God. God is sending you to carry on the mission of His Son, which most certainly involves suffering, as it pictures the gospel.

Once alive again, Jesus didn't stay in the tomb. Jesus didn't renovate the tomb. He didn't add a couch or a bean bag to make it tolerable or more comfortable. Jesus didn't come to life to live where dead people dwell. Jesus came to life to live and by His life destroy death. Don't let your suffering discourage you to the point you stay in the grave. Suffering is not something to just put up with or settle for with some fatalistic attitude. You may be living in death's shadow, but you are alive. Your suffering isn't an unplanned inconvenience; it is a divine invitation to take part in the mission of God—to see death destroyed and life given in the lives around you. God uses suffering to strip away the distractions, the non-life-giving pursuits, the sin, and the death-producing habits in you. God has given you an opportunity to awaken to discovering His unforeseen joy through the suffering that has drastically altered your life. God is on a mission to destroy death and give life—to raise the ruins first in you, then others through you. The genius of a missional God is He takes our suffering, which comes from sin and death, then turns it on its head to reverse sin and death in us and in others. The very suffering that has leveled us, God redeems to raise us.

You are sent by God who first sent His Son, Jesus, who was raised up first on a cross, who suffered and died for the sins of the world, and who was then, three days later, raised up again. This time, however, He was raised for good, conquering death and its shadow. Jesus now gives life as a free gift to all who would trust in Him for it. Your suffering is a picture of His death. And the joy you will experience in your willingness to follow Him through your suffering is His resurrected life in you. Your life pictures a gospel that is never without suffering. A gospel that is never without grace. A gospel that begins with death and whose finish is life. As God raises up the ruins in the midst of your suffering, radically altering you, people will begin to gain glimpses of His power in you. All will see His resurrected life raised up in you. Those who can't look away from your suffering now will soon see the power of His resurrection residing in you; they will see the newness of His life emanating out from you. The ruler over the realm doesn't stop. He won't stop until your life directs people back to Himself.

RULER OVER YOUR REALM

If you choose to accept the divine invitation to be sent by following along with Jesus into the painful mission of God, then you must allow your suffering now to dethrone His rivals, the other rulers in your life. Careers, marriages, children, wealth, possessions, physical endurance, body image, the number on the scale, athletic ability, people's approval, alcohol, sex, food—you name it—can all so subtly become our rulers.

These rulers, to which so many of us submit, are our idols and we their worshipers. We wake up for these things. We live for these things. We sacrifice for these things because we, or the world around us, has convinced us that any one of these listed will bring us true life, if we give them our devotion and energy. Without being aware of it, we pour our energy into these idols, fashioning them with our own hands into sources from which we attempt to derive our life. Yet, in the end, they can't produce life. What we serve and sacrifice for—what we live and die for—are the things that rule us. "Idolatry is not just a failure to obey God, it is a setting of the whole heart on something besides God."[28]

These are the things we gladly submit to and allow to master us because we believe that they will play by our rules when God won't. When God delays, they will give us our quick return. Whatever return we enjoy, however, over a period of time will level out and leave us empty of what we thought was life. We find quick returns in significance, meaning, self-gratification, connection, feeling something, feeling nothing, but none truly satisfying. None truly enduring. They are all counterfeits of the true significance, meaning, gratification, and connection we find in a life surrendered to the true ruler, Jesus.

Power, significance, fame, money, beauty, Instagram likes, alcohol, food, and sex, and their quick returns are not what life is truly about. So in the end, these rulers are nothing but cruel rulers. They give promises of power and wealth—significance and meaning—but in the end, they are the most deceitful despots. In the end, they will not follow through on their promise to grant us a life that lasts. In the end, they will actually rob us of what truly is life. We are just their unsuspecting pawns waiting to be manipulated and ravished by these cruel rulers we serve. Timothy Keller says this of these unfulfilling counterfeit gods:

> Our contemporary society is not fundamentally different from these ancient ones. Each culture is dominated by its own set of idols. Each has its "priesthoods," its totems and rituals. Each one has its shrines—whether office towers, spas and gyms, studios, or stadiums—where sacrifices must be made in order to procure the blessings of the good life and ward off disaster. What are the gods of beauty, power, money, and achievement but these same things that have assumed mythic proportions in our individual lives and in our society? We may not physically kneel before the statue of Aphrodite, but many young women today are driven into depression and eating disorders by an obsessive concern over their body image. We may not actually burn incense to Artemis, but when money and career

are raised to cosmic proportions, we perform
a kind of child sacrifice, neglecting family and
community to achieve a higher place in business
and gain more wealth and prestige.[29]

Suffering is one of God's major weapons to dispose of these rival rulers—these counterfeit gods. Suffering brings us all to a point in which we must decide to which ruler we will surrender over our life in order to truly find it. This is why C. S. Lewis wrote, "The full acting out of the self's surrender to God therefore demands pain: this action, to be perfect, must be done from a pure will to obey, in the absence, or in the teeth, of inclination."[30] The pain makes it painfully clear that we must choose. If we choose to sacrifice these malevolent rulers to make the majestic God the one and only ruler over our realm, we will no longer be pawns; we will be kings.

When suffering comes upon us and we decide to have the courage of faith to face the pain and loss; when we make the commitment to endure the hurt and harsh reality of it all, just like our king Jesus did for us, we—one day—will be rulers with Him. "The Spirit Himself testifies with our spirit that we are children of God, and if children, heirs also, heirs of God and fellow heirs with Christ, if indeed we suffer with *Him* so that we may also be glorified with *Him*" (Romans 8:16–17 NASB).

In Revelation, Jesus tells John to give a message to the church at Laodicea. The message was "Open your eyes." If they would overcome the false sources of this world that promise life in this age, they would rule with Jesus in the next. If the church at Laodicea would realize that their riches and wealth are not actual sources of life, but the sources of their spiritual poverty;

if they would see that their luxurious clothing is not the source of their significance, but actually the source of their spiritual nakedness; if they would recognize that their self-dependency is not the source of their admiration but the source of their spiritual wretchedness, then He would allow them to sit with Him on His throne. Overcoming the temptation to serve these false sources of life, which only resulted in their own spiritual tepidness (like the lukewarm water of Laodicea), they would once again become useful to Him in His mission. The result: they sit with Christ on His throne. "He who overcomes, I will grant to him to sit down with Me on My throne, as I also overcame and sat down with My Father on His throne" (Revelation 3:21 NASB). They shared in His suffering and so they will share in His throne.

However, if these believers would continue to compromise their faith in God as the source for their life for the comforts and riches of this world, they would lose their influence in the world (Revelation 3:16). The things in this world we take as our rulers rob us of what truly is life: knowing God and experiencing the joy of being used by Him to bring Him fame (John 17:3). God is using you and your suffering to bring life to you and fame to Himself. Don't compromise such a high calling from your God for empty sources in this world that can only provide temporary peace and comfort at best.

We are worshipers. This is the core of our identity and for which we were created. If we are not worshiping God, we are certainly worshiping something else. "Worship is first your identity before it is ever your activity. You *are* a worshiper, so everything you think, desire, choose, do, or say is shaped by worship."[31] Paul Tripp continues. "When the Bible says that we are worshipers, it means that every human being lives for something. All of us are digging for treasure. All of us are in pursuit of some kind of dream."[32] Living for, pursuing, and chasing anything as a source, other than Jesus, to satisfy our craving for the life we were created to live leaves us empty. Suffering helps expose all other sources as fraudulent, leaving us to make the choice as to whom or what we will serve.

The most deceiving earthly ruler, to whom we give over our worship and for whom we must constantly be vigilant is not fame or power; it is not money or sex, it is our self. Since being a God worshiper is core to our identity, to worship anything else *we* desire: money, sex, significance, etc., would be to worship our self. It would be us executing our will for our self over our own life. To devolve further into self-worship will accomplish a demolition of the soul. Self-worship is not a reconstruction, but a deconstruction of our identity. This deconstruction leaves in shambles the Christian's calling, sense of meaning, and relationship with God. As long as the soul remains fragmented in the self-worshiper he or she will remain the fraudulent ruler seated on his or her own frail throne.

If suffering has drastically altered your life and you want to make it count, regardless of how impossible and pointless you feel it is; regardless of how many eyes may be fixed on you, then sacrifice yourself as the ruler over your realm. When we remove ourselves and place God in His rightful spot as ruler over our realm, then the impossible becomes possible and the pointless important. God gives it meaning. When we remove ourselves as ruler, we are given meaning. We experience life as worshipers, not fraudulent rulers. We are worshipers whose stories direct others to the ruler over the realm of mankind.

Only when you surrender yourself and get out of His way

will you then see Jesus become the ruler over your realm and these ruins raised up again for all to see. God has invited you to share in His mission by sharing your story. He has given you a story of your very own to tell, but to accept this invitation demands we must first dethrone ourselves. A.W. Tozer put it this way: "In every Christian's heart there is a cross and a throne, and the Christian is on the throne till he puts himself on the cross; if he refuses the cross he remains on the throne."[33] We all, daily, must step down from our thrones and accept the invitation by climbing up on our crosses. "He who has found his life will lose it, and he who has lost his life for My sake will find it" (Matthew 10:39 NASB).

CHAPTER 12

It's Not Over

I T IS NOT OVER FOR US. WE HAVE COME ALONG WAY, BUT IT IS NOT over. This book is not about a miracle ending or to give you a blueprint for your own miracle ending. This book is our story offered up for those who are in the middle of their hurt and for folks who feel forgotten. It is for those fighting and clawing, scratching and climbing. For those whose faith may be failing. It is for the burned-out and the beat-up, the ravished and those reeling. I want you to know I've wanted to give up more times than I can count. There have been days I've just wanted to get in the car, leave my phone behind, and drive away. I don't know where I'd go, but that's not the point. The point is some days I just feel like running away. I think that wherever I end up, I'll be happier. But I know I won't.

We can't run from the calling God has called us to without inflicting more harm. I know there are difficult days that still lie ahead. Hopefully not as difficult as days already passed. God willing, we will just keep moving toward Jesus and so will you. God willing, you and I will keep on worshipping Him without cause. We will keep on faithfully enduring, strengthened by the truth that His grace will sustain us in the meantime, and that our faithful endurance will ultimately direct the attention of others to Jesus.

I am not the person I was when our suffering drastically altered everything. None of us are. We will either be altered for better or worse. This one thing is for sure: suffering never leaves the status quo untouched. I've grown in compassion. I've learned ways to tamper my temper. I've found my triggers and can anticipate the assault on my mind that follows. I have days that are truly supernatural. I had one two days ago. Days in which everything I fear and dread, in fact happen, but still can't touch my confidence in God. Those bad days don't alter me into someone who acts crazy because life is so crazy out of control. I am not a mirror of my circumstances, but instead I'm learning to master the spiritual art of surrender in those mad circumstances. Those days don't alter me for the worse because of the things I've learned and passed on to you in this book.

Sadly, I do still have days that are not close to supernatural. These days, I've come to realize, are the days I'm most selfish. On these days, I put aside all that I've learned because I'm not interested in being like Jesus. I'm only interested in me. The days I don't respond supernaturally are the days I'm more interested in all the things that revolve around what I want, not what Jesus wants for me. The me-centered days are the days I am most reluctant to surrender and follow Jesus when—once again—He is leading me where I don't want to go. On me-centered days I make myself the ruler over my realm. I set myself upon my frail throne and heartily sanction the deconstruction of my own soul as a God worshipper to worship myself. For sure, I have never responded supernaturally to my suffering on the days I default back to seeking my own dream for my life instead of surrendering to God's dream for my life.

All this to say it is not over for us. It is not over for you either. Whether your suffering ends or doesn't, it is not over. God is always working and doing something in us. He's not going to stop pulling out that new creation He's already created you to be. Since you are in Christ you are a new creation. God uses suffering (among other things) to expose the areas in our lives where we are failing to measure up as these new creations. Cancer may be behind you, but that bad day at the office is still ahead. How will you respond to your coworkers behind your boss's back? Today just might be the day you stub your pinky toe. What will come out of your mouth in front of your children? It is not over and will never be over for us on this side of the resurrection.

I've grown tremendously, but I'm not finished. Heidi has definitely grown exponentially, but she's not close to being finished. This is not bad news but good news. When we look at the transformation God has already worked in us, we can be confident He's got more coming. That's comforting. God is not finished with us, and He's not finished with you. So it doesn't matter if you are just starting out on your journey of suffering, right smack in the thick of it, or past it; God is still working. God is working all things to bring about in us—a glory yet to be revealed to us.

> For I consider that the sufferings of this present time are not worthy to be compared with the glory that is to be revealed to us. For the anxious longing of the creation waits eagerly for the

revealing of the sons of God. For the creation was subjected to futility, not willingly, but because of Him who subjected it, in hope that the creation itself also will be set free from its slavery to corruption into the freedom of the glory of the children of God. For we know that the whole creation groans and suffers the pains of childbirth together until now. And not only this, but also we ourselves, having the first fruits of the Spirit, even we ourselves groan within ourselves, waiting eagerly for *our* adoption as sons, the redemption of our body. For in hope we have been saved, but hope that is seen is not hope; for who hopes for what he *already* sees? But if we hope for what we do not see, with perseverance we wait eagerly for it.

In the same way the Spirit also helps our weakness; for we do not know how to pray as we should, but the Spirit Himself intercedes for *us* with groanings too deep for words; and He who searches the hearts knows what the mind of the Spirit is, because He intercedes for the saints according to *the will of* God.

And we know that God causes all things to work together for good to those who love God, to those who are called according to *His* purpose. For those whom He foreknew, He also predestined *to become* conformed to the image of His Son, so that He would be the firstborn among many brethren; and these whom He predestined,

He also called; and these whom He called, He
also justified; and these whom He justified, He
also glorified. (Romans 8:18–30 NASB)

Although our glory is not yet, it is as good as done. And though our glory is not yet, it doesn't mean we can't discover the unforeseen joy hidden in the suffering that precedes it. Just as death precedes resurrection, preceding glory is suffering. We cannot share in conformity with His glorious image without first preceding it by sharing in His glorious suffering, which He asks us to endure. By understanding His suffering to be missional, you will start to gain a sneak-peek into this glory which is yours and is coming. Since glory is preceded by suffering, we "rejoice in our sufferings" knowing what incomparably follows. The Greek word used for *rejoice* here in some translations of Romans 5 is the same for "boasts" or "brags." We brag in our suffering. We exult the story of our suffering, because it honors Christ when attention is directed to His resurrection power at work in us, to alter us into His image through our suffering. Though we don't go looking for suffering, we rejoice nonetheless because it means glory, for God now and us later.

The promise of finally conforming to the image of Jesus, coupled with the truth that nothing can separate us from the love that drives Him to work all things to bring this about, comforts us. Nothing will keep you from His loving desire to grow you into a mature, radical follower of Jesus who thirsts today, more and more, for the glory to come.

What then shall we say to these things? If God *is*
for us, who *is* against us? He who did not spare

His own Son, but delivered Him over for us all, how will He not also with Him freely give us all things? Who will bring a charge against God's elect? God is the one who justifies; who is the one who condemns? Christ Jesus is He who died, yes, rather who was raised, who is at the right hand of God, who also intercedes for us. Who will separate us from the love of Christ? Will tribulation, or distress, or persecution, or famine, or nakedness, or peril, or sword? Just as it is written,

"For Your sake we are being put to death all day long; We were considered as sheep to be slaughtered."

But in all these things we overwhelmingly conquer through Him who loved us. For I am convinced that neither death, nor life, nor angels, nor principalities, nor things present, nor things to come, nor powers, nor height, nor depth, nor any other created thing, will be able to separate us from the love of God, which is in Christ Jesus our Lord. (Romans 8:31–39 NASB)

Through Jesus, and His love for us, we are strengthened to overwhelming conquer any suffering that may come our way. Nothing can stand in God's way of loving you and, through that love, ultimately altering you into the image of His Son, Jesus. And our present sufferings, though detested, are not worthy to be compared to the glory that supremely follows. It will happen one day. However, you must make the choice. Do you want to begin enjoying the down payment of that glory now or wait until that day? Will you fight God on His plan to work all things for your good now? Will you harden your heart toward Him? Will you refuse to let Him be the ruler over your realm? Or will you allow Him to have His way in this life with your life? Will you lay down the life (which deep down you know you've already lost) so that you can pick up the life He's laid down for you to live? If you do, you will begin to taste, more and more, the unforeseen joy now of the glory that is promised to come.

JUST KEEP MOVING

We have a family motto—"Austins Never Give Up"—and with it is a recently added appendage, which is "Just keep moving." A few months ago, I joined a gym. In the months leading up to my joining a gym, my anxiety had grown out of control. I was so convinced something bad was going to happen I wouldn't let anyone leave the house some days. There were days the anxiety was so debilitating that I couldn't imagine ever working again or having a life. That hopelessness then left me unable to get out of bed many days.

I joined a gym because I was scared of what the stress was doing to my heart. I can't run or do anything else that most do for cardio, but I can ride a bike with one leg. I recently had read Charles Duhigg's *The Power of Habit*. In his book, Duhigg discusses keystone habits having the power to start a chain reaction, either in organizations or in the life of an individual. Keystone habits are small, easy changes that have the potential to disrupt long-held habits hard to break.[34]

I've joined gyms before and, like many, never got real traction. So I was going to make one keystone habit—something easy that might have a great ripple effect. My keystone habit was every Monday I would cycle for ten minutes. On Mondays because it is easier to make myself get in a gym on the front end of the week rather than on the back end. Ten minutes because I was out of shape, but mentally I would be able to suffer ten minutes then go home.

It only took two trips to the gym before I was cycling three days a week for twenty minutes. After a month, I was three to four days going for forty-five minutes. Now I ride close to an hour, which is about all my butt can handle a bike seat. Having a keystone habit doesn't make it easier, but it gets you in the door and gets things moving. That's what I needed. Once in the door, my anxiety fueled my workouts. I would go hard for forty-five minutes to an hour and still be amped up afterward. However, once my anxiety got better, my workouts were less energized.

Anyone who has ever worked out knows the mental battle that rages. *I'm not feeling it today. I don't want to be here. This workout isn't as good as the last. This hurts.* I fought through these same common negative thoughts of wanting to get off the bike and go home. One day, after my anxiety no longer fueled me, I was struggling to get into the workout mentally that I was already physically pushing through. It was at this point when a thought popped into my head. *Just keep moving.* I told myself that I've already hit my Monday ten-minute goal so everything else was just a bonus. So *just keep moving.* It doesn't have to be pretty. It doesn't need to be as good as the last workout. You just need to be here, be present in the struggle, and the only way to do that is to just keep moving.

I found if I just kept moving, then eventually, somewhere in the workout, I would have a breakout moment. The breakout moment is that moment when in the muscle fatigue and mental weakness the endorphins kick in and carry you the rest of the workout. When I feel my body turn the corner from fatigue to fully engaged, it reframes my perspective from wanting to quit to giving 110 percent. I go from one thought away from quitting, and getting off the bike at twelve minutes, to being covered in sweat, pedaling full force at the sixty-minute mark. All because I kept convincing myself to *just keep moving.*

You may be one thought away from quitting. You may be one thought away from deserting your God. You may be one thought away from walking out on your marriage, picking up a bottle, or pulling the trigger. Don't. *Just keep moving.* It hurts, and turning the corner from pain to persevering seems like a complete impossibility, but it is not. The only thing impossible is finishing the race of your faith if you stop moving and give up. You've shown up. You're reading the book. You are present and in the fight, so just keep moving. Things will get better. They may get worse first, but you will have your supernatural breakout moment and God will carry you through. Just keep moving.

I just turned a corner writing this. I don't want to write today because my thoughts are consumed as such: *This book is terrible. No one is going to read this book. If people do read it, you're too vulnerable and people will just trash you. People will trash Heidi. Just keep moving. You can't even remember writing class growing up and now you're writing? Who are you kidding? Just keep moving. You are a nobody, an obscure failure, in your midthirties with no career. You have nothing to show for yourself. Just keep moving. Just keep moving. Just keep moving!* Even if all these thoughts I tell myself are true, at least I showed up. At least I didn't stop. I'm still moving. I'm answering the call to take my suffering, which feels personal, and make it missional. We are not giving up. We are leveraging our suffering for God's glory. You too, right now, *just keep moving.*

When you can't get out of bed because the depression and hopelessness are so heavy, just keep moving. Tell yourself you are going to put one foot on the floor, maybe just a toe, then get back in bed. It may seem like nothing, but it could hold the potential to a chain reaction that gets your thinking to turn the corner. Just keep moving. Whatever it has to look like for you, just keep moving.

If you have lost someone close to you and you can't picture your day without them, the chair may be empty, the house a little quieter, and the little reminders of that person everywhere, remember you are still here. With every subtle reminder, don't fight the pain. Acknowledge it, grieve it, and move your thoughts to gratitude. The little reminders hurt, but the grief is actually helping you to keep moving. Grief hurts, but we can't run from it. We have to face the loss to keep moving. This is our brain's way of saying goodbye. "In grief, we *learn* to live without the one we love, but the reason this lesson is so hard is that we first must *unlearn* the idea that the person exists and can still be relied on."[35] Just keep moving from one little reminder to the next, thanking God for the memories. Just keep moving.

Ultimately, we want to do more than just move. We want to be moving toward Jesus, the ruler over our realm. When you honestly cannot wrap your mind around why God has allowed you to suffer, just keep moving toward Jesus. Often we are driven by our limited understanding of our circumstances to make sense of our faith. In reality, what we should do is follow the maxim of Anselm of Canterbury, who in *Proslogium* wrote about "faith seeking understanding." With a maturing faith—an enduring faith—we allow our suffering to push us into seeking a deeper understanding of who God is, and even better, who God is to us. This, of course, will ultimately result in us having a deeper, more robust relationship with God. A relationship that strengthens us to endure; a relationship that empowers us to just keep moving.

Keep showing up to church. Keep having real conversations with other believers and with God through prayer about how you feel. Keep reading your Bible, even if it is just one verse a day. Don't stop. Just keep moving toward Jesus. "Draw near to God and He will draw near to you" (James 4:8 NASB). Whatever onslaught you are suffering just keep moving toward Jesus. Before you know it, you'll turn the corner. You will have a supernatural breakout moment and will feel the power of God carry you. When you are fatigued and weak, God will lift you and energize you. Just keep surrendering in worship without cause, and through it, He will radically alter you into looking, more and more, like Jesus.

In those early days, when I would find my wife altered, when I would find her voice slurred and her eyes heavy with deadness, when I would find her completely altered into something so scary and someone so foreign, I never dreamed that where a personality disorder was drastically altering our lives, God, in His grace, was standing ready to radically alter us.

EPILOGUE

I'm sitting here at my kitchen table; papers are strung out everywhere, and my last sip of coffee, like always, now cold. I'm easily distracted today. I keep finding myself staring out the window at my backyard, which desperately needs to be mowed. The grass has sieged my children's tree house, slowly ascending and covertly climbing the fortress beams of the swing set. I mow, and it comes back. I mow, but it always musters a counterattack, a resurgence. The Oklahoma Bermudagrass is relentless.

Heidi's borderline personality disorder is also relentless. Sitting in the deafening silence of my house, I wrestle with doubt over my own ability to go the long-haul if I must. What if Heidi never fully gets a grasp on her BPD? The thought of a never-ending and always unpredictable wave of attacks on our life, on our sense of peace, is engulfing some days. There have been some serious spiritual highs at times writing this book. There have been times I felt like I could fly I'm so doped with hope, regardless of whatever earthly outcome may threaten.

Now is not one of those moments. For whatever reason, I'm grounded. I'm scared. Will the assaults stop? Will the suffering persist in its relentlessness? Whatever progress we make, will there always be a counterattack? Will BPD always muster a resurgence?

Someday, very soon, my children will be too old to play on their tree house/swing set. They will grow up, and I won't be able to protect them from the same hurt I feel watching their mommy struggle with the thoughts in her head and the desperate, and often destructive, escape she sometimes finds. I hope to God by the time our children can read this we will be beyond all this and onto the next adventure. I hope they'll have a hard time believing this isn't just a work of fiction.

Right now I'm trying to practice the very things I've been writing to you about. I don't share this to demoralize you or to discourage you, but to be real with you. There will be ups and downs; there will be decisive victories and crushing defeats. I wish once the lesson was learned, its practice automatic. It is not. It is a daily grind. I can say it gets easier as your faith matures (and it does), but as a friend of mine recently put it, the flesh never quits whispering; it never quits wooing us away from Jesus. And it is true. Sin is the most seductive of sirens in our suffering, wooing our flesh away ever so subtly toward anything and everything other than following Jesus for our relief.

I was on the bike earlier today, desperately pedaling to outrun the racing, hope robbing, thoughts that battle ruthlessly for the high ground of my mind. I had to keep telling myself, "Just keep moving." And so, that is what I'm going to do. I'm going to just keep moving toward Jesus, regardless of the earthly outcomes that threaten. I'm going to pray my children never know the hurt, but I'm going to end my prayer with "Not my will be done, but Yours." No *but* and no *just not*. Just Your will not mine. Period. Because as sick as I am of all this junk; as fed up as I am right this moment, I'm choosing to surrender my wants for His wants.

I will fight back the assaults my anxiety wages on my sense of peace. I'll mow down, again and again, the foreboding thoughts that lay siege to the buttresses of my mind. I'm choosing that no matter what others do to me today, I'll be ready to respond with grace and compassion because that's how Jesus has always responded when I've caused Him harm. I'm ready, today, to worship without cause and be altered more into the image of the One who has guaranteed to keep me and protect me for the heavenly outcome of the resurrection. A day, once and for all, when we will no longer know suffering, but great joy.

> Now to Him who is able to keep you from stumbling, and to make you stand in the presence of His glory blameless with great joy, to the only God our Savior, through Jesus Christ our Lord, *be* glory, majesty, dominion and authority, before all time and now and forever. Amen. (Jude 24–25 NASB)

NOTES

1   C.S. Lewis, *A Grief Observed* (New York: HarperOne, 1996), 25.

2   Martin Seligman, *Learned Optimism: How to Change Your Mind and Your Life* (New York: Vintage Books, 2006), 44.

3   Erwin W. Lutzer, *An Act of God?: Answers to Tough Questions about God's Role in Disasters* (Carol Stream: Tyndale, 2011), 54.

4   Jerold J. Kreisman and Hal Straus, *I Hate You—Don't Leave Me: Understanding the Borderline Personality* (New York: TarcherPerigee, 2010), 62.

5   Dr. Seuss, *Oh, the Places You'll Go!* (New York: Random House, 1990).

6   Caroline Leaf, *Switch on Your Brain: The Key to Peak Happiness, Thinking, and Health* (Grand Rapids: Baker Books, 2013), 72.

7   Paul David Tripp, *Suffering: Gospel Hope When Life Doesn't Make Sense* (Wheaton: Crossway, 2018), 46.

8   Brené Brown, *Daring Greatly: How Courage to Be Vulnerable Transforms the Way We Live, Love, Parent, and Lead* (New York: Avery, 2012), 69.

9   Ibid., 12.

10 Brené Brown, *I Thought It Was Just Me (But It Isn't): Making the Journey from "What Will People Think?" to "I Am Enough"* (New York: Avery, 2008), 24.

11 Randy Alcorn, *Does God Want Us to Be Happy? The Case for Biblical Happiness* (Carol Stream: Tyndale Momentum, 2019), 34.

12 Paul David Tripp, *Suffering: Gospel Hope When Life Doesn't Make Sense* (Wheaton: Crossway, 2018), 66.

13 Erwin W. Lutzer, *God's Devil: The Incredible Story of How Satan's Rebellion Serves God's Purposes* (Chicago: Moody, 2006), 54.

14 Randy Alcorn, *If God Is Good: Faith in the Midst of Suffering and Evil* (Colorado Springs: Multnomah, 2009), 417.

15 Charles Stanley, *The Gift of Forgiveness* (Nashville: Thomas Nelson, 1991), 108.

16 Ibid., 134.

17 Jim Wilson, *How to Be Bree from Bitterness: And Other Essays on Christian Relationships* (Moscow: Canon Press, 2007), 11.

18 Melody Beattie, *Codependent No More: How to Stop Controlling Others and Start Caring for Yourself* (Center City: Hazelden, 1992), 34.

19 David Sheff, *Clean: Overcoming Addiction and Ending America's Greatest Tragedy* (New York: Houghton Mifflin Harcourt, 2013), 109.

20 C. S. Lewis, *The Problem of Pain* (New York: HarperCollins, 2001), 94.

21 Dietrich Bonhoeffer, *The Cost of Discipleship* (New York: Touchstone, 1995), 89.

22 A. W. Tozer, *The Root of the Righteous* (Camp Hill: Wings Spread Publishers, 2006), 69.

23 Lysa Terkeurst, *It's Not Supposed to Be This Way: Finding Unexpected Strength When Disappointments Leave You Shattered* (Nashville: Nelson Books, 2018), 150.

24 *Blue Bloods*, "Second Chances," episode 11, January 5, 2018.

25 Joni Eareckson Tada and Steven Estes, *When God Weeps: Why Our Suffering Matters to the Almighty* (Grand Rapids: Zondervan, 1997), 202.

26 Paul David Tripp, *What Did You Expect? Redeeming the Realities of Marriage* (Wheaton: Crossway, 2010), 33.

27 Timothy Keller, *Walking with God through Pain and Suffering* (New York: Dutton, 2013), 284.

28 Timothy Keller, *Counterfeit Gods: The Empty Promises of Money, Sex, and Power, and the Only Hope That Matters* (New York: Viking, 2009), 171.

29 Ibid., *xi-xii*.

30 C. S. Lewis, *The Problem of Pain* (New York: HarperCollins, 2001), 98.

31 Paul David Tripp, *What Did You Expect? Redeeming the Realities of Marriage* (Wheaton: Crossway, 2010) 33.

32 Ibid., 34.

33 A. W. Tozer, *The Root of the Righteous* (Camp Hill: Wings Spread Publishers, 2006), 72.

34 Charles Duhigg, *The Power of Habit: Why We Do What We Do in Life and Business* (New York: Random House Trade Paperbacks, 2014), 100.

35 Norman Doidge, *The Brain That Changes Itself: Stories of Personal Triumph from the Frontiers of Brain Science* (New York: Penguin Books, 2007), 118.

Printed in the United States
by Baker & Taylor Publisher Services